GW00690905

A Breath of
Country Air

Part Two

Henry Williamson on his Ferguson ploughing Hang High, c. *1938*

A Breath of Country Air

by
Henry Williamson

Part Two

The Henry Williamson Society
1991

This collection first published by The Henry Williamson Society 1991

Text © The Henry Williamson Literary Estate 1991
Foreword © Robert Williamson 1991

Standard edition ISBN 1 873507 00 3
Limited edition ISBN 0 9508652 9 X

All rights reserved. No part of this publication may be
reproduced, stored in a retrieval system, or transmitted, in any
form or by any means, electronic, mechanical, photocopying,
recording or otherwise, without the prior permission of the
copyright owners.

Typeset by Cambridge Photosetting Services
Printed and bound in Great Britain

CONTENTS

CONTENTS

ILLUSTRATIONS

FOREWORD

by Robert Williamson

The two sets of articles contained in the second part of *A Breath of Country Air* were written at a time of great stress, both in the world, and in Henry's life. The Second World War had ended in the summer of 1945, and Henry's farming venture closed at Michaelmas of same year. It is hard to imagine a greater traumatic time for anyone, especially that of a sensitive artist, and yet as the last year on the farm unfolds there is only the very slightest hint of the tiredness and bitterness brought about by frustration that Henry undoubtedly felt. Instead we are treated to reflections and memories of the West Country, humour and an amused view of himself as shown in *Running in the rain* and *So we spared that tree*. There is the voice of the visionary in *Revolution on Britain's farms*, a voice much more in keeping with the ideas and views of today than 1945, and there is the closeness and empathy he felt for his youngest son. With Rikky he could once again delight in the natural world, and through his wanderings on the farm, remake the discoveries that he himself had made as a small boy in the woods around his home in Kent. These two were much together in the last year on the farm, as the elder children were away at various schools, and it was the beginning of the break-up of the family.

But perhaps the most poignant of all the articles are those concerning the sale of the farm. My mother has said of that time that Henry was looking for a way out, and was glad when she told him that she could no longer go on. Here was the chance for him to go back to "What I wanted to do more than anything else in the world – write." How fortunate for us that he was able to do that for the rest of his long life.

Through the *Quest* serial I have been able to re-enter the family history. My Uncle and his growing family stayed with us at Botesdale, and an RAF family helped to fill the rambling old house. Being away at school, the holidays were greatly enjoyed, and Henry has captured the mood of these holidays, now that the strain of the farm had gone.

Henry was writing full time, but also spent time in the West Country and London. The faithful Silver Eagle Alvis had been given away to a friend, and Henry bought a 1936 Aston Martin for these journeys. In a nearby village a similar car was being prepared for the Belgian 12 hour race, and Henry got to know the owner/driver Jock Horsfall. Rikky and I once spent a terrifying afternoon being driven round a disused airfield in this car, as Jock tuned it up for the race. There were visits to nearby Snetterton racing circuit, where the Aston Martin Owners Club held race meetings. Henry enjoyed these and once got in by airily declaring to the official on the gate – "I'm driving" as he pi'oted the family Ford 8 through.

Henry's Asto . Martin gave him both great pleasure and trouble. He spent much money on keeping it going, and always blamed the previous owner of selling him a dud. In all fairness, the previous owner, whe n I met years later, still maintains that Henry swindled him over the sale. Thus each has gone down in the other's family folklore as the archetypal car villain – caveat emptor!

During the five years at Bank House, Henry wrote or re-wrote various books, including *The Phasian Bird*. Notes for chapters 23 were written during a performance of Bach's Mass in B Minor, given in the chapel at Blundell's School. Both Rikky and I were in the choir, and Henry filled his programme and those of his neighbours with his impressions. After the performance, he congratulated the music master Jimmy Hall, and told him of the inspiration he had found in the music. He showed him the notes he had made with the comment "The true artist is always working – I can never stop."

We moved from Bank House in 1950, and Henry went back to the West Country to prepare for the great task of the *Chronicle*. The period of his 'Quest' was ended.

But for us, the enjoyment of those times is just beginning, and I invite you to enter the final year of Henry's farming venture with gentleness, so as to savour to the full that which has been created for us by "the true artist."

INTRODUCTION

Part two of *A Breath of Country Air* concludes the series of articles which were published in *The Evening Standard* with those written in 1945. As before, they appeared on the Monday features page, and are one of the few items in which mention of the war is minimal. No doubt this was the brief given to Henry Williamson, so that city readers could escape to the bucolic charms of farm life (there were few indications in the delightful prose that the writer was waging his own grim battle).

Nightly the headlines, and much of the rest of *The Evening Standard*, were shouting in the boldest of type the advance of the Allied armies in the battle for the Rhineland, marked each day by the towns captured: Cleve on 13 February, followed by Goch, Udem, Xanten. Forgotten names now, but every one the scene of bitter street fighting. February 14, and the public were first made aware of the bombing of Dresden and consequent firestorm. By March the collapse of Germany was accelerating, while a month later the war in Europe was nearing its close. There was an increasing optimistic speculation in *The Standard* over a post-war Britain, and perhaps it was not just a coincidence that Henry's piece of 23 April was given the title *Everything looks brighter now*.

His contributions were held over during the ensuing three weeks, for events imposed their own demands on strictly rationed newspaper space. On 30 April Berlin fell to the Russians, and Hitler killed himself; a further fortnight and Germany had unconditionally surrendered, and a Britain exhausted by war was celebrating VE Day.

Britain's exhaustion was mirrored by Henry's own, and at the end of May he seems to have returned to North Devon for a break of several weeks. A General Election was held on 5 July, the result a foregone conclusion; the Beaverbrook-owned *Standard* confidently predicting a Conservative majority of 100. It took three weeks to gather votes from Britain's forces overseas, and Labour's sensational landslide victory was not announced until 26 July. One suspects that Henry was too worn out and preoccupied with his own problems to care: in *What shall I do about harvest?* (24 July) he reaches a nadir, in which his tiredness, and perhaps a first recognition of defeat, are allowed rare expression. His despair would have deepened a few days later, for the 'malevolent glint' of the first atomic bomb devastated Hiroshima on 6 August.

In October Old Hall Farm was sold, its implements auctioned, and the Williamson family moved sixty miles south to Botesdale. That this was a fresh beginning for Henry is evident from the second section of this book, *Quest*. Fifteen linked pieces, they appeared in *Woman's Illustrated and Eve's Own* between February and October 1946. The evocatively named magazine, which matured over the years into today's *Woman*, announced the series to its readers as 'Henry Williamson's story of his Quest for happiness and security.' Henry, typically, preferred 'harmony and truth.' He was given a full page, and each article was illustrated with sketches. The extra space meant that Henry could develop his themes more fully than he had been able to in *The Standard*.

Without the worry of the farm, his writing has a new serenity, and in these engaging pieces he tells most sensitively of the family's reunification, and their first year at Bank House. They form a satisfying and enjoyable postscript to the finished story of a Norfolk farm.

J.G., 1991

ACKNOWLEDGEMENTS

The Henry Williamson Society gratefully acknowledges the permission of the Trustees of the Henry Williamson Literary Estate, *The Evening Standard* and *Woman* to reprint this collection. The Society's thanks also to Robert Williamson for contributing his foreword, and to the Trustees for their permission to reproduce photographs from the archive of the Literary Estate.

REFLECTIONS OF AN OTTER

The story of the gibbon ape which after living with Japanese soldiers in the jungle crossed to the British troops and tried to live with them on equal terms, is not one that I, speaking from my limited association with wild birds and animals, read with scepticism.

According to *The Times* correspondent on the Chindwin front, the ape soon learned to drink tea in the mess, smoke cigarettes (after realising that it was "not done" to tear them up and chew the tobacco), and to lie low when shells and mortars came over.

The ape was wounded, and allowed itself to be evacuated with other casualties. Before this it had shown that it disliked being laughed at or imitated by going away when this happened and "sulking."

Imagination, reinforced by experience – the faculty of creating within the mind pictures of what happened – tells me that these reported facts *were* facts. I have always believed in the essential kinship of human beings with animals, and in a lesser degree with birds, and even with fish.

Human beings have developed the faculty of calculation, and through the use of imagination can often see the future, or rather the trend of individual personal future. Man can reflect; but is it certain that animals are without the power to reflect, within their limited lives, or world?

Try to imagine a party of "civilised" whites, say an expedition to "bring 'em back alive" for the purposes of a film display for entertaining credulous Metropolitans, finding that aspiring gibbon ape in that same jungle before the war. One can imagine the laughter as it ate lipstick taken from a chemical blonde, as it gulped cocktails, tore up paper, and showed artistic temperament of an ape unsure of itself in artificial surroundings.

But among men whose understanding is shorn of the artificial and often decadent characteristics of white civilisation – men simplified by the hard realities of war – a natural ape would be able to feel that confidence which comes from "feeling at home."

As trust of its new companions came to it, so it would develop an admiration for their ways and doings, which it would naturally imitate. I say naturally, for imitation is one of the main instincts of life, equal probably to the instinct of curiosity. (These two instincts are not yet sufficiently appreciated by educationists.)

Curiosity leads the ape to watch, to observe, to imitate. Its incipient social instinct (derived from care of its young) is rebuffed when it is laughed at for making a mistake, for being "crude." The ape has feelings, and to imitate its behaviour is to hurt its feelings, and to mortify temporarily its social instinct.

The so-called secret of success with animals is to know that they have feelings, to treat them as equals in an emotional sense, to be at home with them. Any good horseman knows this.

I used to know a man in the West Country whose knowledge of wild English animals was exceptional. He had otters, badgers, and foxes he had tamed. They used to follow him about. Once the badger went roving and got in a rabbit trap, and as I mentioned in an article a few weeks ago, when it was set free by him the "brock" ran to him, rose on its hind legs, hid its head against his knees, and whimpered while he held its wounded paw.

This is no "humanising" of animals, a term often used by scientists whose knowledge of them is confined to laboratory experiments.

I have carried a baby otter about with me, feeding it from a bottle; a small brown animal, kitten-like, which used to sleep up my coat sleeve and on my shoulder. It grew up to be a swift low-running animal, shy of other people, and from which tom cats immediately ran yowling.

One night while it was hunting eels down a small valley stream, and had gone into a small wood, probably running a rabbit's scent, it got caught in a gin and three of the claws of one front paw were lacerated. The strength of its struggles was terrific as it rolled and contorted, biting the iron, while blowing and hissing; and when at last I got it free it disappeared.

I found its spoor on sandy scours of other waters, and once up by Pinkworthy Pond in the middle of Exmoor.

One day, I think, this early friendship and the odyssey of the search for the otter, culminating in a nine-hour hunt and the drowning of a hound in tidal waters by the dying otter, will make a startling film. In most films of wild life I have seen, the directors miss, through inexperience, most of the marvels of air, water and earth which are there for those with eyes to see.

January 1, 1945

THE GLITTER ON THE WATER HAS GONE

At the beginning of an ice period any stone or stick or root or fern which is sprayed or wetted near a water-fall or other obstruction in the stream slowly becomes coated with ice.

Brambles which have pushed through the riverside alders to find rootage for their young green tips, and have found instead the surface of the stream, become slowly clubbed with ice. This ice, as in the case of ferns and roots, is made of innumerable layers of thin water.

The club of ice on the bramble tip becomes slowly heavier, the bramble draws backward and forward less quickly from its spring of alder branches, until the weight of ice extends it diagonally downstream.

Water piles up against the moored ice-bottle, which loses its slender neck and becomes as though thickened by an inexperienced glassblower.

All living things feel some sort of pain at times; and if the weight of ice does not tear the bramble from its bush, or a thaw release it from torture, next spring it will hang there red and coarse, unbudding until finally it withers and dies.

The fly-fisherman wading there will break it off, lest when he throw his delicate olive-dun there at the next noontide rise, it should get caught up.

The frost holds. Brittle plates of ice form over still water by the sides of runs and eddies. Icicles, still called cockabells by some Devon children, hang under the falls where before water trickled very slowly. These seal the trickling places; and water trickles elsewhere, making new cockabells.

Rocks and shoals lipped by water thicken with ice, and gradually the river level is raised. Pieces of ice break away and are carried down to the next eddy, where they lodge or ride slowly until welded into the local ice, strengthening it.

The slow solidification of eddies and still stretches by the shallows causes the runs to run faster, creating thereby other reactions or eddies or water-resistance.

Moving water is governed or has its existence by the same natural laws which govern all the movement called life. Life is action, movement, progress as well as reaction, otherwise resistance or conservance; but action, movement, progress are of the Spirit which gives life, as the biblical poet observed.

The plates of ice holding frost strive to convert running water, which lags thereby and weakens in its purpose for life. Grasses and waterside rushes help to hold the ice. Towards mid-day the sun in a clear sky subdues the arrogance of rime, melting first the hoof-marks of cattle and deer which wander along the banks.

Above the fall the water raised by the dam of ice suddenly presses a way through. Dead leaves churn with sand in the pool below. Soon the warning sound runs down with the fuller stream: the ice cracks and whimpers, some plates breaking away to ride down tilting and heaving.

The shadowed piers of the bridge below hold the floes, while frost instantly begins to work on them, sealing them to the stonework.

Soon the sun is behind the trees on the western hill-line. The grass droops again as the rime settles. The weir is seen to be thicker with ice. Thin layers of water run over that ice, thickening it.

It is very cold by the river, and now I see passing in the water clots of semi-opaque, jelly-like substance, slightly resembling the jelly of frogs' eggs without the dark specks which are the eggs. It is like colourless algae; but no algae grow in cold water.

The stream is filled with the slush. It is slush! Evangelical ice has conquered: the water is slowly being converted, slowly losing its joy of life, its natural brightness.

The slush moves slower than the water, impeding it, striving to become static against every stone and snag, clinging to the plates of ice, which welcome it; and the running water diminishes.

At night the Dogstar is green above the south-eastern horizon; water-sounds are dulled, except where the fall roars. A mist moves over the water, becoming denser and pressing nearer the surface towards midnight.

The mist of slush drags slower in the faint-hearted stream: the mist of iceblink drags at it from the still air: only the falls roar with lessening power: and then, in one moment, the splayed glittering of the Dogstar on the water has gone. Ice lies from bank to bank.

January 8, 1945

SEASCAPE

The ravens of the headland are thinking of the nest on the cliff edge where for many years their young have been reared. Every year since I first saw them as a demobilised soldier with five years of war behind me (forever behind me, as I thought then) a nest has been made on that overhung ledge, about 20ft. from the grassy edge of the cliff.

The five eggs are usually laid in February, and the young birds driven away from their parents' territory – extending along a mile or two of coast – in April. The ravens have been there for centuries.

As I lay in the weak sunshine on top of the cliff two peregrine falcons flew swiftly over, stooping upon each other in play. The stoop of the falcon is a thrilling sight. I could hear the buffets of their pinions as they met in the air, crying the shrill spring chatter of joy, falling for a second afterwards with wings as though wrapped around each other.

The female was a third as big as the tiercel, or male. I hoped to see a stoop upon one or another of the herring gulls, but the gulls knew they were not dangerous to-day. Sometimes a grey gull left the floating, wailing throng and pursued a peregrine: the sharp blue-black wings flickered and the gull was immediately outflown.

The stoop or dive of the falcon is magnificent. The bird shuts its wings and dives head-first at so steep an angle that it appears to be a perpendicular drop at double the pull of gravity. It is not a swooping down, but a driving downwards of sinew, muscle, bone and feathers compressed between the barb of wings, directed by fearless power and concentrated in one terrible thing – the full intentness of the eyes.

The cormorants on the black rocks below, holding out their umbrella segment wings to dry, watched them with anxious jerks of thin black heads.

After their play the peregrines rose on the wind until they were six hundred feet above me, "waiting on their pitches," in the term of falconry. They remained still in the buffets of the wind. Their wings were bent back, sharp and dark, the head blunt, the tail thick, short and stocky.

Whereas the windhover, or kestrel, can remain still in a soft, favourable wind by constant delicate shiftings in its leaning, the peregrine appears to cut its stance in a half-gale by suppressed force.

A small bird, probably a finch, came fluttering in from the sea, a frail-looking thing of flight, fluttering to reach the land after its rough journey in the wind. Had it come from Lundy, or even from Ireland? One of the falcons tipped up, flickered blackly, *swished* down, and curved up again without a wing beat to its pitch nine hundred feet above the waves and six hundred above me. A perfect parabola; time, seven seconds. The small bird struggled on, and the smaller tiercel then stooped. He too missed. His speed carried him almost into the waves; he swept up likewise without a wing beat, and again two black stars were motionless in the gusty wind.

I waited in dread for the finch, but after the first colossal dives the falcons ignored it, and it arrived at the cliff-face to crouch on a green hummock of sea-thrift near me, its beak open as it panted, as I saw through my glass.

The cold wind blew up the cliff, shaking the dry, colourless grasses of last summer; the finch began to draw its flight quills through its beak, to set the filaments; the black stars, with never a flicker, turned down the wind and slid across the sky and out of sight along the north side of the headland.

The cormorants on their whitened rock below seemed easier; a general preening of neck-feathers began, shaking of tails, and flapping of dull wings. The raven sat still and huddled on his scaur; the lower part of his body was hidden by rock, but his eye saw all that moved.

One of the cormorants jumped off into the wind, swung round, and beat its black wings steadily over the sea, just above the wind-streaky troughs of waves. Another launched itself into the wind, followed by a third and a fourth, while a newcomer appeared flying over the waves to the rock; it luffed into the wind, alighted on a perch just quitted, and opened its wings, as I thought, to dry after its underwater fishing.

Its head seemed unusually large, and, looking through my glass, I saw that it had caught a flat-fish, which it could not swallow. It worked its wings as it gulped, half ejected the fish, and gulped again; then settled down with the tail sticking out, waiting until there was more space in its bulging crop.

On the sward of the cliff-top lay many small feathers of gulls; and among the winter-broken hummocks of sea-thrift, which cover the point of the headland with pink, wind-trembling flowers in May, were fragments of blue shells, crab-claws bleached white, fish-bones, and sometimes a rabbit-bone, thrown out of the crops of gulls which rest here when no human figures move against the sky above their green slopes.

January 15, 1945

OWLS IN THE THATCH

I read the other day that the Ministry of Agriculture had asked farmers to open the owl-holes in old barn-walls, slits left usually high in the gable-end, for the birds to fly in and out. This brought back at once a memory of days after the last war when I lived alone in a Devon cottage, which was mine for five pounds rent a year.

It was cob-built, and stood, one of three sharing a common roof of thatch, below a churchyard wall in the village. My cottage was the eastern one, and under the ridge of thatch – high up at the end of the gable – was a dark triangular hole.

The wall was two feet thick, built of mud from the clay soil, bound with cowdung and straw; this was called cob. The cottage was said to have been built in the reign of King John. The owl-opening had been there since the building of the cottage.

I took the cottage, which had been empty some years, because a pair of white owls had their home over the ceiling of the bedroom. I used to watch them silently flying out, like great white and yellow moths, as the evening light was stilling towards twilight. I painted on my cottage door the outline of a barn owl, with my initials below its clawed feet.

The white owl symbolised for me the peace and beauty of the countryside, the spirit of the wild, of star-light, the sunsets of the Atlantic, the soft murmur of the stream arising in the quiet village night, and the eternal truth of nature. After five years of war, and with responsibility only towards my writing, I had found freedom.

I made some notes in those days, and was amazed by the number of small rats and mice a family of barn owls would eat in a season.

The barn owl reared its family in relays. The eggs were laid at intervals on the ceiling, which was several inches deep, all over, in mice fur and small bones. The owl swallowed its prey whole, afterwards casting up from its crop a pellet containing the indigestible matter. These pellets, tens of thousands of them, during the years had covered the entire lath-and-plaster ceiling.

On April 17 the first egg was laid. Two more appeared on April 18 and 19. During the second week of May these eggs hatched, and two more were laid. The owlets were blind, partially naked, and they made a shrill, lisping noise for food.

By midsummer there were three fully fledged owlets over my ceiling; two snow-white bundles with long, hooked beaks and immense claws; two tiny lisping parcels òf skin and blindness; and two fresh, white, chalk-rough eggs.

A month later there were five grown owls, four adolescents, two babies, and one addled egg. I took the egg, washed it, blew it, and my son has it now.

To get this information I used to creep up a half-rotten ladder belonging to a neighbour, heave myself over the ledge and crawl head-down to the worm-eaten rafters of the rickety ceiling. The grown owls shrieked at me and flapped away into the far gloom, the adolescents ran away, the babies blinked. But what astonished me was the number of dead rodents lying near the nest. I counted twenty-seven mice, nineteen young rats, two sparrows and forty-two field voles.

The time was then 10 a.m. At 7 p.m. when I climbed up nothing remained of them. Ninety animals eaten by eleven young owls in nine hours! And this, moreover, during the time of rest and sleep.

Lying on the grassy slope of my garden wall, near a young thorn grown from a seed dropped by a bird, I watched at twilight the old birds at work. They flew from the disused coach-house beyond the churchyard where they roosted by day. The sun was lowering itself into the Atlantic when they came with the first mice.

They were greeted with hissing cries, and frantic bumping and scrambling noises; then one by one they unfolded from the dark angle of the cob wall like white blooms against the reddish-purple tower of the Norman church, and floated in silence eastward over the tombstones to the glebe field.

At intervals of from three to six minutes either the cock or the hen would return with a mouse or mice, held in beak or dropped foot. Their children seethed in noise like a great saucepan boiling over, the prey was cast among them, and the bird sailed away, sometimes pursued by screaming swifts.

Throughout the summer nights the toiling owls brought food for their young. When they fed themselves I know not. They worked on for about an hour and a half after dawn.

For their family the barn owls caught about 150 rodents every night. From April to the end of August I reckoned that nearly 10,000 mice and small rats were brought to the owlery in my roof. I left the cottage five years later.

January 22, 1945

WHITE STREAMLINE

Snow lies on the hills, and the trunks of trees have a narrow verticle stripe of frozen sleet facing the blizzard from the north-west. The woods are gaunt under a rime-ringed sun; the white fields are dotted with the wandering tracks of hares and rabbits.

Last week the stubble by the Hanger Wood was chequered by black heaps of dung, set out regularly in straight lines from hedge to hedge; well-rotted dung, pleasing to the farmer's eyes. Now they are white like the rest of the field.

What a day that was, the day of the blizzard. Coming home in my car the engine seemed to be seizing. On a level road it was slowing up; I had to change into second gear, while the petrol indicator showed that the tank was nearly empty.

I stopped to look at the dipstick, fearing lack of oil. And opening the door I found that my mouth was almost blown open by the blast which was threshing the thorn-hedges and whipping the telegraph lines.

Hastily I got back into the car, while many icy jets of air explored my body, and all vision through the windscreen was excluded by sleet. Through a side window I saw the white, multi-snaking winds pouring over the earth. I watched a straw-stack moving across a field.

Through the glass I watched straw after straw leaving its place in the stack, pale yellow straws riding away in the wind. One followed another, swifter and swifter, until the entire stack seemed to be in disintegration. Ten acres of oat straw, possibly ten tons, value £40, when I passed that way two hours previously; and now, after ten minutes, a tall and distant hedge of straw gleamed golden in the light of the sudden low-shining sun. And across 300 yards of frozen furrows the yellow straw was spread.

I went slowly through a world modulated by a streamline and flowing white design. Every stone, every swede in a field of roots, every dead thistle and stick – all things which had lain on or out of the earth – was shaped as though for a journey into space. Everywhere the wind, as it weakened from hurricane to gale-force, as it subsided to the cold shocks of a half-gale and thence to a steady breeze, settling to a gentle flowing of air before yielding the earth to silence, had left the snow in white streamline behind all ground objects.

Broken and neglected things subduing the spirit before (all men dream of fairer aspects) – broken abandoned cart, rusty plough, fallen gate-post, dinted petrol cans abandoned by soldiers – were modulated by the white and flowing shadows of the snows. The flowing masses of the snow streamed from the fields and in places filled the road from hedge to hedge.

Dare I try to get through those drifts? As I walked forward to explore, I noticed in one place the curious corrugated effects of the snow, and was startled to hear coughing coming as it were out of the earth. An entire ewe flock was buried under the lee of the hedge.

I knew the danger to the ewes of suffocation in that massed heat. I decided to risk continuing along the road. It was easier than I had thought, and along the road I met the shepherd, with sacks tied round his legs, and, after telling him, I went on my journey.

What a sight when I got to the meadows of my farm, lying below the road and the river. The distant sea, piled up by the wind against the tidal sluice-doors, had stopped the flow of the river, which now was within a few inches of lipping over its banks. But the wind had stopped in time, and even as I peered the water began to move downstream.

I thought of thorn-logs blazing in the open hearth, of a deep leather armchair, slippered feet, and a mug of tea. The last of our sugar-beet had gone to the factory: no need to think about that. For the moment the farmer's mind was clear.

But stay! Had I not promised to take young Rikky, the only child now left at home (the eldest boy, as farm steward, is no longer a child), sledging on the hills?

With a vision of the small boy waiting disconsolately with the sledge, I went on home, and putting away the car (about a cupful of petrol left in the tank) I went indoors. There were the thorn brands flaming on the hearth, my leather chair before them, my slippers beside the bellows, the kettle steaming on the iron crook, the teapot on the table.

The afternoon was already darkening: what about poor Rikky? Then looking across the valley to the white hills I saw in the dusk a small black shape descending fast, watched it hit the well-known bump and turn over, and two dark figures – one small and one big brother – picked themselves up and with laughing cries ran down the hill to the sledge at the bottom.

January 29, 1945

FOOTPRINTS TELL THE TALE

While the world was white we had the illusion of uniformity and order. The snow crunched underfoot, one's footsteps were clear and defined. It was obvious where birds and animals had walked, too.

The first thing I noticed was the number of hare tracks. They were easily distinguishable from the lesser rabbits by the length of the lollop, and by the long thrust of the hindleg.

They had regular ways, entering the fox covert wood by the south-east corner, coming from the frozen sugar-beet toppings which lay on the field.

The hares found shelter in the wood, as they crouched in their forms in the snow, by the edge of a bramble patch or under the fallen branch of an elderberry. All the tracks leaving the wood were in the south-west corner, where the trees sloped down to another field which was sheltered from the wind.

As the winds increased many hares went down to the meadows, which lie low beside the river. The bank of the river extends in a horse-shoe shape from west to east, and under its lee, by the thick bushes of thorns and brambles, the hares foregathered. Their quatting places were immediately apparent by the reddish-yellow patches on the snow.

It was under that bank that we flushed a woodcock, then another, a third and a fourth.

One flew up almost from our feet with a faint whinnying cry, as though of fear or anguish; we watched its dark pointed wings flickering away.

Another arose with a whirring of wings which was like that of a partridge, and we saw its long beak as it turned in the air and pointed down two hundred yards farther on, across the river, by the three wheat stacks which had been badly dishevelled by the gale. Hardly had it pitched when an owl arose and on slow, yellow-pink wings began to flap in silence along the river bank, over the rough grasses of the farther slope.

This was not the white or barn owl which lived in the ruined towers of the Hall. We knew that bird, which had a gold back streaked and laced with ash-grey. This owl was pink on the back.

All kinds of rare birds come to the coast of North Norfolk, and many, alas, are shot.

Our boots crunched on down the river bank, while snipe arose in twisty flight and screaky cries before us. All the meadow was frozen, and they found feeding only by the riverside. The heron, of course, saw us long before we saw him; he arose on lazy, wide wings three hundred yards away, and flapped away to the marshes.

When we got to where he had been standing – easily visible by the long broad arrows of his toes – we found the big silvery scales of a roach on the bank. He had evidently been banging it to kill it before swallowing, and also rubbing it in the snow.

By the Carr we saw the best sight of all: the broad five-toed "spoor" of an otter, beside the mark where his low body had dragged through the snow.

Every now and again he had turned on his neck and shoved himself along on his back, enjoying the feel of the snow against his spiky hairs.

After a look at the river we went back over the ice and crisp snow of the meadow. We really came down to look for an axe I had mislaid somewhere while clearing an old hedge some months before.

It was not in the hollow tree where usually I kept it, out of the rains. But the otter was, and with a hissing and scrambling, his whiskered flat face staring before he vanished, he fell out of the dry ledge where he had been sleeping, and we heard him pushing along the ditch.

"Ooh!" exclaimed Rikky, his eyes wide, his cheeks pink. "An otter in *my* tree!"

He was overjoyed, for on that ledge he had been wont to sit out of the rain when exploring that mysterious country.

February 5, 1945

JUST GREW!

One Sunday afternoon towards the time when owls were shaking their wings preparatory to launching themselves to their evening hunting, two weary people might have been seen passing through a gateway of a Norfolk farm.

All that Sunday the two had been going up and down the field, in the cold and dour March day, drilling oats.

Three bushels of oat-seed still remained in the drill. It was unwanted seed. It would be useless for hens.

Left in the drill, that seed would be a nuisance, since the next drillings would be of barley; and oats in malting barley were mere weeds.

Through the gateway they entered the top part of another field, steep and narrow between woods, where a crop of oats and tares, drilled the previous autumn, for spring sheep-feed, had failed. The field was almost bare. At no time in living memory had that part of the field ever grown a crop.

The farmer was a newcomer to the district. His ardour to succeed where others had failed was only matched by his inexperience. Trying to cure that "cold old land," he had in previous years sown mustard there. It grew on poor land, and was generally grown for cover for pheasants, or a relish for ewes before mating time. The farmer's sheep had eaten it down and manured the land. He had ploughed this under in due course, and had again grown mustard. Then he had ploughed and drilled wheat. It had failed. He had then spread tons of rich black mud over the field, ploughed it in deep and drilled oats and tares. This crop failed. The farmer decided to empty the unwanted bushels of oat-seed on that land.

The shoes of the drill made lines about half an inch deep, into which the grain trickled.

The oats drilled in the adjoining field in the normal way, after ploughing, harrowing and rolling and a dressing of artificial manure, came up; so did the oats carelessly dropped on the "cold old land." The yield was thrice that of the other field, and each sheaf was too heavy for a boy to lift.

Next year the farmer grew barley there without ploughing. He merely scratched up the old oat stubble with a cultivator and let it lie on top to rot. After drilling the seed he rolled it down hard. The barley crop was the best on the farm.

This made him think. On another field was a patch of chalky land where nothing grew. He dug some leaf-mould out of the woods, and spread it there. It was quite a thin layer, looking like black pepper on a slice of bread. It was merely stirred into the soil with a harrow, and oats drilled on it. These oats were nearly as fine as those from the "cold old soil." On land which, ploughed, grew nothing!

I was that farmer. And when, therefore, I read *Ploughman's Folly* (Michael Joseph, 8s. 6d.), a book which declares that the act of ploughing, of turning in weeds and debris too far under the vital surface of the land, is responsible for all the silted riverbeds in the U.S.A., for the millions of acres of soil erosion, for most plant diseases and crop failures, at once a responsive chord vibrates within me.

When I read that the author, Edward Faulkner, has grown bumper crops by leaving all the decaying matter, old dead weeds, rotting straw, etc. – the plant food – on the top of his fields, chopping and shifting and mulching this top soil with disk harrows only before sowing his seeds or setting out his plants – and this on land abandoned as unfertile by other farmers – I begin to wonder if he hasn't "got something."

Mr. Faulkner, farmer and son of a farmer, says that dung, or green crop ploughed under for manure, stops the capillary action of moisture in a soil; it acts as a damp-course in a house-wall. Above the damp-course is dryness.

When that humus breaks up into plant food – invisible potash, phosphates, etc. – the rains merely carry it downward to be lost in the subsoil. Lacking this essential porous plant-food on the surface, plants starve, and rains run off with silt and sand – erosion – and this has been going on for hundreds of years, all over the world.

February 12, 1945

GLIMPSE OF SPRING

Every Wednesday and Saturday afternoon I get away from the cares and worries of life – for farming and the raising of a family both have their little difficulties – and hide away by myself in the woods on top of the Home Hills.

There I enjoy myself for an hour or two, in my own quiet way. Yes, there's room for two where I am going, if you care to come with me.

You will want an extra coat. Yes, I know the sun is shining just now, but about 5 o'clock a cold air moves up the hill, as though an invisible iceberg were moving over the slopes. You will be glad of the coat then.

We cross over the river by the bridge, and come to the farm. On the pond many duck are splashing, enjoying the spring-like sunshine. They are a cross between Runners and Aylesburys, and there are two wild mallard with them. We collected 400 snails from an ivied wall yesterday, in the garden, and they soon finished them.

Here's the Home Hills. Used to be rough, tired, old grass; now as you see, it is ploughed. This is the second ploughing. The "flag" or old buried turf, is rotted. Take a bit in your hand; see that brown, thin, writhing insect? Wireworm! They will play Old Harry with the oats we drill here soon.

I have not dug up a square foot of ground and counted them, thus reckoning how many to the acre, but I should think there are 500,000. How many plants of oats will that insect army bore through, and so cripple? I'll sow peas in the oats, in case the oats fail badly. Wireworm generally do not eat through peas.

Here is the edge of the wood. We'll enter above, on the top. I want you to see the view. Isn't it a different world up here? Miles of sea, marshes, and fields; and down there the Elizabethan home of Francis Bacon, beside the church. Woods, river, and meadows; just the same as it was before the war, and will be after the war. England, my England!

From this plateau you see, the other way, the red roofs of the village. The drabness is lost up here; down there, one passes along a narrow road with decaying flint walls rising beside it, shutting off the view. That's because it was built along the bank of the stream. But from here one sees only the red-tiled roofs against the fields and the trees, and the reality of the small dark cottages does not press upon the consciousness.

16

Here's the wood. Look, a mark on the earth by the bank. A fresh footmark! Someone has been before us. Who can it be? Let's follow his tracks. They are soon lost in the leaves of oak and beech blown on the mould under the bare trees. There are pines here, as well as elm and oak. Those speckled marks on that tree-trunk are made by a woodpecker, chipping the bark for the grubs boring underneath.

What's this? It looks like a gigantic squirrel's drey fallen out of the tree. Branches of elderberry and pine and sticks are piled against the trunk of an oak, in the form of a rough wigwam. Straw is roughly woven (pleached is the word) round the sticks, to shut out the wind. Inside is a wooden box, to sit on. The straw keeps out the wind. This is where we are going to sit – our "hide."

Let us follow through the wood before we settle down. There's plenty of time; the pigeons won't be flying in to roost yet. Speak quietly; creep along. I've retained this habit from boyhood, and of whispering in a wood. You see and hear much more then. Hear those tiny tweedledee cries? That's from a pair of cole tits, who live in the wood.

Come forward, slowly. See anything? There, just in front. Somebody chuckling? Who would think a man was sitting inside that tangle of thin elderberry sticks? His brown clothes harmonise with the oak leaves on the woodland floor, his cap is brown, the pipe in his mouth breaks up the pink area of his face. Meet "Scroggy," old soldier, Mons Star, perfectly camouflaged in his "hide." His double-barrelled gun rests across his knees. His cartridge belt hangs on a branch. Back to our "hide."

You sit there, on the straw. If you hear the beat of wings, don't look up. The pigeon circles the wood first, scrutinising before he swings in to alight. Let him settle. Others will follow. Then slowly raise the gun, get a bead on a bird, select another for the second barrel, while being careful to see that no twig is in the way of the shot.

No, you take the gun; I am quite content to sit here, to let myself get the feeling of the wood, the peace of it, to see the tiny glinting heads of the first nettlepoints rising among the leaves, and the green seedlings of the woodland plants with their first two small open leaves.

See! A tiny bird like a brown leaf has flitted mouse-like into our hide. It is a wren.

Later on in the spring young Rikky will tell me he has found a

round nest, made of moss and leaves, with a hole in the side, in my
old pigeon-hide in the oaks. The bird flits out again. In a day or two
we might hear him singing, for spring is on the way.

February 19, 1945

View from the pines on Castle Hills

PATIENCE AND RHYTHM

One of my enjoyable occupations on the farm is the clearing of old trees and undergrowth, and later seeing the land come into cultivation again.

A neglected pasture changes its character; the wrong plants or weeds soon dominate, and there comes a time when little new annual growth is made, because the roots are congested and matted.

The only thing to do then is to plough the tough mat under, take a crop of corn or roots for a few years, and finally to re-seed with new and improved strains of grasses and clovers.

During the past week I have been felling some hilltop thorn-trees which were over a foot thick at the base. They were old, gnarled, and powerful.

For some years I had rather dreaded the job of throwing, stripping and burning those big trees on the crest of the hill. So I put it off again and again, telling myself that I ought to be writing – my real job – instead. I did a lot of writing, enjoying it, neglecting exercise and gradually growing stale; and the more stale I got, the more reluctant was I to work with my body. But at last it must be done; the land must be cleared.

The first thing was to get the axe sharpened. It had a 7lb. head and its edge was rounded. That meant no pleasure in using it; all hard blows and little progress. So I set to work with a file and scraped away all one evening.

When the shoulders of the axe-blade were thinner by about half an ounce, I put an edge on the blade with a stone until it would cut a piece of paper cleanly drawn along its edge.

The sap was beginning to rise in the thorns. The buds had swelled slightly, and showed lighter in colour. It was the right time to fell the trees.

Done properly, tree felling is a pleasant job. The axe sinks into the wood, the swinging undercut sends the chip flying. You cut a large nick the way you wish the tree to fall; then start to cut from the other side. Practice makes your sinews obey your eye exactly; each throw of the axe brings satisfaction; and thus the tree falls in a surprisingly easy manner.

Then, after only the least pause to commend yourself, you step among the branches and "strip" them from the main trunk or trunks. Lovely, clean slanting cuts across the pink wood! These branches you lug out, and remove with a light foreshortened swing their lesser branches.

Nothing is wasted. The main trunk, split by wooden "beetle" and wedges, is cut into lengths for the circular saw; beside them, neatly laid out, the lengths of branches, also for the saw. The chips will be gathered up later, when dry, for kindling.

The art of all country work lies in developing, at the start, the slow rhythm of physical work; this can only be done by practice. In fact, the nervous system has to be broken-in to such work; its reluctance overcome; and if you are an "intellectual," if your mental reactions are quicker than your body, with its unpractised muscles and sinews, you will suffer in the adjustment. But, once the slow, happy, natural rhythm of manual work is learned by the body, it is never forgotten. It is patience.

If a child learns it early in life, it will have learned the lesson of harmony early. But only the body can teach the mind patience. Harmony is the balance of mind and body, not one outracing the other, which is human maladjustment, unhappiness, self-seeking.

In a few minutes I am going to the hills again. My axe lies below, beside my old Canadian mackinaw coat, with the stone-sharpening "slip" in one worn pocket, and a bottle of cold tea in the other. I shall not fire, with the aid of old tractor oil, the heaps of thorns I have laid on the stumps, until all the trees are down; I know exactly what I am going to do. If I start burning now, it will check the anticipation of my sinews, which long to wield the axe until the last old "bull-thorn" cracks and crashes.

Fire-making is another rhythm. The fires will come last of all. The charred roots will rot in the ground; we will get them out next year. The potash I shall scatter with a shovel, and where it falls the golden oats of August will have heavier heads of corn.

In my garden are five small walnut trees; when the hills are seeded down to grass again, I shall plant out those trees, on the site of the thorns, staking them against the cattle which will graze there.

February 26, 1945

SPRING IS A LITTLE EARLY

The lilac is coming into leaf by the red tiles of my small barn. Near the latticed window of the larder the daffodils are breaking into flower. Our weekly washing waves gaily on the line in the garden. The hedgehog has woken up from his hole in the ivy-bank. The giant walnut tree is beginning to swell at the buds.

Primroses are out, and snowdrops are an old story. Wild sweet violets on the sunny bank under the Fox Covert are scenting the air. Down in the green meadow Italians are cutting the osiers of the willow stubs, tying them into bundles for basket-making. They sing as they work, and their work is good. Never have I seen such neat bundles tied by osiers twisted into a rope. But shall we be able to sell them?

What an early spring! Will we have to pay for it later on? When I was a boy staying in Buckinghamshire, one April, I remember a snowstorm which came and filled the nests of thrushes, blackbirds and hedge-sparrows. The eggs were frozen in ice.

Richard Jefferies wrote that the walnut was a silly tree; that was why in olden times men who wanted the wood for gunstocks and the nuts to eat with their wine planted them on eastern slopes of hills, for the early east winds to discourage their easy exuberance. If its leaves "burn" or wither, the later crop of nuts is liable to be diminished. A tree breathes through its leaves.

It is too windy to light my fires of waste wood on the Home Hills. I have thrown all the old thorns, cut them into sizable lengths for the circular saw (winter 1946-47) and they lie in cords or piles ready for stacking down below. The stumps in the ground are ready covered with heaps of slashed branches, piled up like eagles' nests, ready for firing with the aid of old tractor oil.

I have learned that a fire made in windy weather burns through the heap, cutting a tunnel with the horizontal flames; the mass of twigs and branches above remains unburned. But on a still day the flames arise in tawny cones and the embers cook the stubs in the ground, preventing them from sending up shoots. The roots die, and the next ploughing we get them out without breaking the ploughshare.

Last week we threshed our last stack. The Italians came to help us. Some had not used a pitchfork before; but they did their best. It rained that day; the corn came out damp. We had to send 80 sacks away, each of 1½ cwt. (it was oats) to be dried artificially.

Threshing is hard work in the best of conditions; in the rain it is a fearful job. But the more it rained the more the "Eyeties" sang. I saw one man using a pitchfork on the strawstack (which is made of the threshed sheaves) as though it were a broom. As he was giving himself extra work, I attempted to show him. With an unhappy face he cried, pointing all around: *"He a-show me, corporal a-show me, boy a-show me, everyone a-show me, now you a-show me! Me a waiter, me carry dishes, me no farmer, you a-see?"* The situation was, as our horse-man remarked, "A rum'n."

All the mice and rats of the neighbourhood appeared to be in our stack. Weasels, too, those hunters of mice. A local dog had a fine time, so did a basket of local kittens. I see with pleasure that an owl now lives on the beam of our barn.

Rats migrate; you can clear them out of your premises, and the next night a couple of hundred move in from elsewhere. Stoats and weasels are increasing rapidly, and so are jays and magpies.

I have seen a large rat, three or four times the weight of a weasel, cringe when hunted and sit in the middle of a lane and squeal as the weasel who has been trailing him reaches him; to circle round his crouching form until it runs lightly on his back and bites him behind the ear. The rat dies without struggle. The weasel is the most courageous animal in the world, as the rat is one of the most intelligent, dirty and selfish.

It is time the spring corn was going in, but I am half afraid to say we have not started yet. When I see my neighbour drilling corn, and I not begun, it gives me a twist of alarm. But we will get by.

The wet autumn held up the ploughing, then the snow delayed us again. One-third of our cornland will not be ploughed this year; we are going to use the disk-harrow, to make a tilth on top, and drill the corn on that. If we plough, the furrows will dry out, and we shall lose the subsoil water.

The disk-harrow covers six times as much land as the two-furrow plough, and makes the seed-bed in the same operation. Forty acres of corn should mean £800 gross of barley at harvest: what if the disking is insufficient? But it won't be; I have no doubt of it, and that is three-quarters of the battle.

Twenty-four thousand barrels of beer depend on one man's decision! What a responsibility! I feel a great sympathy for Mr. Churchill, for I do not have a House of Commons to account to; not

RUNNING IN THE RAIN

An Airborne soldier on leave walking over our farm hesitated when he saw me on the road between two of our steep fields.

I was in a hurry. It was 3 p.m.; at 4.20 p.m. the post left the village and I had an important despatch to write. I was running, my shoes were wadded with brown soil. I had not shaved, I wore neither collar nor tie, and I had not yet had any breakfast or lunch. As I knew what the Airborne soldier wanted – to see a pal who worked on our farm – I told him to follow me. I would take him to his pal.

He had to run to follow me. Before, he had been proceeding with leisurely calm, down the lane; maroon beret at correct angle on head, neat khaki uniform showing the creases of tailor's iron on sleeve and trouser; leather anklets and boots well polished.

Six months ago he was a village boy who markedly had not believed in the rules of tidiness which the Boss had tried to institute, but after six months, what a change in his bearing!

Why was I running? There was a battle on; I was fighting on two fronts; I was general ordering operations, quartermaster, chief of staff, tractor instructor, and correspondent.

But let me go back a little while to explain. For days the weather had been dry, and everywhere, as far as the eye could perceive from the high ground, tractors and teams of horses were crossing and re-crossing hundreds of acres of brown earth. England's corn was going in, while the going was good. Indeed, the going was too good in places, the exceptional weather had dried out the spring-ploughed furrows of our best field, and the worst had happened: the furrows had gone off as hard as curbstones in the whipping east winds. And what seeds *could* grow in a "tilth" resembling broken curbstones?

We had concentrated, before the too-dry spell, on another field where a fine seed-bed had been worked up.

First the heavy rib-roll to crush the sweetly disintegrating furrows, breaking to powder at the touch; then the disk-harrow to work down the soft lumps; then spiked harrows to rake them over; a light roll behind Gipsy the mare, and there in the March winds was a tilth worth a king's ransom.

We started sowing barley yesterday morning and got 14 of the 20 acres in by nightfall and went home as the bombers were droning about the clear, dusky sky, and said we would finish that on the morrow. As for the other field, well, we would have to wait for a "dag

of rain" to soften those furrows like curbstones, to "catch them right"
as they were half-moist, half-dry.

At 5.55 a.m., as I was lying awake meditating my despatch to you
this week, heavy drops of rain began to beat on the glass tiles in my
bedroom roof.

I listened anxiously, wondering how much rain would fall. If a lot,
then the drilling of the first field would not be completed; if rain fell
for a week, or the field lay too wet to sow, the first lot of barley would
be up; that would mean a patchy harvest, a poor mixed quality of
barley. If it were to be "a nice little dag of rain" (as they say in
Norfolk), then the hard furrows of Fox Covert might be workable.

Which would it be? In a few minutes I would have to give orders for
the day. At 6.55 a.m., in rain falling steadily, I "issued" the orders.
Then I sat down to meditate my despatch. At 7.35 a.m. the rain
stopped and so did my meditation.

At 8.15 a.m. as I was about to eat breakfast the sun was shining
through a misty sky and the wind was beginning to blow. The "little
dag" of rain would soon blow out of those clods! I must not lose it!

Then the telephone rang, and I learned that ten tons of fertiliser
would probably be arriving round about 11 a.m., and men would be
needed to unload it. I was thinking about this when Rikky came in to
say the bullocks had broken out and were heading for the airfield.

Then I remembered that the corn we had threshed in the rain,
which had gone away to be dried, was due to arrive at 10 a.m.

The battle was joined!

The sun shone, the wind blew, the blackthorn was suddenly white
as I dashed by on my bicycle, the whitethorn leaves were emerald
green, yes, yes, but what about those clods? On the field, I hastened
across its acres, wondering if it would do more harm than good if . . .
Harrow? Roll? . . . And would the new Italian driver know what to do,
a nice intelligent fellow, worked in the Fiat works before the war. . .
But was the other field too wet to drill? I hastened to it.

It wasn't too wet! Can you hear me, shouting across the valley?
(Aircraft over all the time.) What, you can't start your tractor? All
right, I'll come. Look Luigi, you spik Ingleese? Bon, mein amigo,
pronto, accelerando, little dag go, in wind, see? You go there buddy,
up and down, okay. Have a fag, chum. No gum, chum.

It was after getting in the bullocks that I met the immaculate and
sweetly strolling Airborne soldier on leave. "The battle," I said, "is

joined. It goes well. The clods are working down surprisingly nicely into a sweet tilth. By this afternoon it would have been too late. The barley goes in nicely in the other field. The fertiliser won't come until to-morrow morning; nor will the corn! Good morning!"

Did he think I was crazy? Well, here is my report, finished at 4.15 p.m. I hope you will forgive me if it isn't about very much.

March 19, 1945

THE SPIRIT OF WILD PLACES

It is pleasant to walk on the meadows and to feel the heat of the sun being absorbed by the plants of the wheat. The radial heat of the sun is drawing life from the earth; the leaves of the corn shine in the wind. A hare starts from its day-dream behind a tussock of the old ploughed turf which the ploughshare and the heavy roll could not bury last September, when we ripped up the stubborn matted turf of a century and tried to turn it under to rot, and to feed the wheat sown there.

I stand still, watching the hare dash through the hedge and up over the slope of the grass field beyond. Will he stop and squat on the summit, watching me with his great eyes turning for a backward glance, though his head will be pointing away from me? I stand still; he flees on, the very spirit of fear.

Lapwing are rising and tumbling over the clods and lines of green plants in the uneven field of corn.

Soon they will lay eggs, and it will be difficult to find them as we harrow the wheat, pick them up and set them down again; perhaps, if there is time, marking the place with a stick, so that the roll following in a few days' time will not crush them.

We love the lapwing; in their voices are the very spirit of wild places, of freedom from the cares of civilisation. The lapwing's cries are the voices of the elements, of water and air and the truth of the sunshine.

During my first year of farming, when things were often most difficult, one of my happiest moments was when a ploughman told me that it was the local custom to care for the lapwing's nests, to protect the eggs though it meant a little trouble as the successive implements passed over soil being worked down for a seed-bed, then the sowing and the harrowing and the rolling to follow. To me it was the natural virtue of men working in the elements who were uncorrupted by the spirit of the market place.

Why care for a mere bird? Why not take the eggs and eat them? Who would know if the harrow dashed the eggs to fragments? But the sorrowing mother bird would stand mournfully about the place, day after day; the man behind the horses would know what she was feeling. To have knowledge for another's plight is to have sympathy; to identify feelings of another with your own; and so the act of neighbourliness, of unselfishness, towards another, although but a bird, is entirely a natural one.

Human life cannot always be judged on a basis of the facts, or truth, of the jungle; and there is something superior (and it is not mere sentimentality) to the activities of the little ego which must strive against its neighbour.

A man walking and working alone thinks along many lines of thought. When the habit of slow patient work has been acquired, such as day after day following horses in one field after another, such work gives its own satisfaction.

Life becomes simple, as for the lapwing feeding on the wheat, probing for wireworm and other insects, standing in meditation beside a tussock of half rotted turf, then as the joy of spring surges in its being, running with wings uplifted and soughing into the sky, to wheel and roll and rise again, spinning and twirling, dashing down to earth while uttering the wildly sweet *see-o-weet, see-ooo-weet!* to its mate picking rootlets and grasses and laying them in a slight hollow, sitting down to turn them in her beak, thus making the rough outline of a nest, in which, in due course, the brown, black-blotched pointed eggs are laid, and brooded over with such passion as the eggs are tucked between the thighs of the bird, and its temperature rises to flow into the life forming within the shells.

What fidelity of the father bird! Ever on guard, he dashes at birds far superior to himself in strength and cunning – the carrion crows, gulls and rooks which fly over the fields, searching for eggs to suck. But the fury of natural righteousness possesses the lapwing, and that moral force gives him strength to buffet them away.

Up and down he flies, crying wildly and sweetly when the danger is passed; his note changing as another enemy approaches, to be dived on from above and discomposed from below as the greenish-black and white pinions swish within an inch or two of the marauder's head. Lapwing, plover, or peewit, call him what you will; he is the Celtic spirit of our English fields and meadows.

March 26, 1945

SO WE SPARE THAT TREE

The corn is green, the willows are in leaf. On the meadows the grass is growing, and the wild duck broods her eggs in the nest in the clump of reeds in the dyke.

Spring is here, and we say to ourselves with hope that it is the last of the wartime springs.

Down by the dyke, near where the wild duck sits on her eggs in the reed-clump, the old blackthorn hangs down its branches, its trunk writhen and bent over.

Beyond the bank where it grows lies a wood, called the Carr. Tall sycamores and ash trees grow there.

Every winter, when the times come to pull the reeds and other water vegetation from the dyke, I look at the bare, black, shapeless blackthorn and say that it ought to be cut down.

That is the farmer's viewpoint. Then I think of the tree which has grown out from the shade of the wood to find the sun, of its ceaseless struggle to live, of the beauty of its blossoms, so fragile and white, breaking from among the savage spines and writhen branches, so sudden and tender a sight after the bleak winter.

No, we mustn't cut it down. For seven years now we have seen it put forth its springtime blossoms. It is a friend.

I remember a thorn in bloom on the downland slope before the Hindenburg Line, and a young soldier lying in the fixed immobility of death near it. It was just after the battle of Arras, and I had walked alone past the outpost line and into the grassy *glacis* extending before the wire-belts, drawn by the sunshine and an instinct to meditate alone.

Seven years afterwards I went back to that place and sought to find the tree. But I could not find it.

It was a day like the one of my memory; larks were singing, the sun was shining, the air was still. Yet though the war was over, I could not recapture the tranquillity of peace I had found there on that afternoon of 1917.

In those post-war years there was not the understanding between soldiers and civilians as there may be now. There was a division in thought between the articulate survivors of battles and those who had not felt the fear and anguish of those unimaginable moments.

Here is the old blackthorn, its lower branches combing the water, its fragile white blossoms open to the truth of the sun. Far away on the road beyond the meadows men are walking slowly, enjoying the festival of reawakened earth, of the manifestation and truth arising again at Eastertide. They, too, have seen comrades fallen in the mortblast of machine-guns, and the rest of their life is gentleness that comes from understanding.

But how about this new lot, this small group of boys crouching over a fire in the corner of the Carr? Let us sit down and observe them.

There are five boys, they have a fire of sticks, a kettle is about to boil. Obviously it is some sort of a camp. Two of them, though hardly five feet high, wear uniforms of khaki; they are school cadets. Another smaller boy wears a uniform of his own designing; a green velvet school cap with an enormous cock pheasant's feather rising out of its peak. He sits near a heap of metal, scrap gathered from an airplane crash. Another wears an American khaki cap with broad peak pointing upwards. The fifth boy is hatless.

Like the others he wears a home-made knapsack which is supposed to be a parachute casing. Now you have it – they are paratroops dropped down here, and having a meal by a fire.

What is the future of these innocent small men?

The world is now sweating out its frustrations on the battlefields. Mankind learns only through pain. And beyond the pain is the simple virtue of the elements of clear and simple living, like the bloom of the blackthorn hanging over the mirror of the water.

April 2, 1945

WINGBEATS ON WATER

At the bottom of the cliffs lies a clitter of rocks fallen in past ages from the sea-worn edge of the land. Seaweeds and shellfish grow on the lower rocks.

The way up the cliff is steep, but not dangerous. There are many footholds on the embedded pieces of fallen rock, half hidden by grass and ivy. At the top the land breaks vertically.

The sands two hundred feet beneath, with their pools and watery ribbed hollows, and the jumbled heap of dark-edged rocks, now appear immediately beneath one; to miss a hold by hand or foot would mean a series of bounding rolls down the slope and a final crash on the rocks.

But it is no time for imagination; grip the turf and pull yourself over, and rest in the long grass.

I watched the jackdaws flying against the wave-broken blue of the sea. Some pitched on the ivied crags farther west, and watched me. For months they have passed and repassed this place without a cry, or a check in their steady wingbeats, or flown with the rooks in the fields, each for itself, but one morning, soon after the rooks had flown to their ancestral trees, each pair to claim a nesting site and to caw satisfaction to the sky and the rest of the colony, the daws held aerial tourney over the fields and the sea.

They twirled and dived, they hurled themselves upon each other, they imitated the flight of other birds, they croaked deeply like ravens. Pair by pair they fell out of the revel. The place became precious in the glow of ancestral memory, the cliffs grew bright with detail. The fire of spring was kindled and lit their pale blue eyes. Every gull was an intruder, every passing of the delicate-winged kestrel a menace to their dreams. Now their eggs are laid in the deep crannies of the rocks.

Primroses are blooming among the wet tussocks of withering coarse grass; the leaves of the bluebell plants are sprouted thickly on the slopes above the cliffs. As I sat there all the daws flew out with a rush of wings that conquered the noise of the south-west gale, with cries of *Jank-jank! Quank!*

The gulls farther along the cliff broke into a white wailing swirl over the sea. Looking around, I saw two herons flying below me, their broad grey wings easily visible against the brown sands. One followed the other.

The leading bird was probably the heron I had seen many times flying from an inland pond to the brook; he had a regular round of fishing stances. Now, with his mate following him from stance to stance, the dull routine was gone from his life – until the young in the tree-top nest by the lake began to grow, when it would return again – and his world glowed with the fire of spring.

They wanted to cross the headland, but the wind was too strong. With his mate he had probably taken the easy way, a glide down the land until he came under the wind. And gliding near the sands and the long unrolling white of the shallow sea he had swung round and the long beat upwind had begun.

The big hollow wings beat steadily, lifting into the wind the narrow bodies with the attenuated legs held stiffly straight behind. They rose higher and higher, above the line of the house three miles away across the Bay. They flapped on, while many gulls and daws, blown erratically by the gale, swirled about them.

One minute, two minutes, three minutes my head was lifted more and more, but the herons made no forward progress. Other gulls joined the pestering flock, some of them following the herons until at last the grey birds turned downwind and turned to cross the base of the headland over the fields; but when they met the wind they were thrown up again and forced at last to glide down to the sands, where they pitched.

April 12, 1945

A WALL BESIDE THE SEA

Like most of the stone walls built on the high fields of the Atlantic seaboard country, a certain wall where often I have sat and watched the rip of the tide over the Leap beyond the headland, is beautiful in spring with lichens.

The wall is a few yards from the precipice, and guards the stony fields from the winds and furze and brambles.

The wall, irregular with much repairing, has no mortar between its flakes of ironstone, but only soil. Where the wall meets the full force of the south-western gales, which send the spume and the salt spray flying over the edge of the precipice – three hundred and ten feet above the sea – its base is thickened and fortified by clumps of sea-thrift, in mounds of green strength or brown ruin according to age.

The south-west winds have driven the seeds of the pink thrift into the crevices between the stones, and there they have sprouted, finding a hold in the inner earth with their long tentacle roots.

Rabbits dig tunnels in the wall, but their burrows are not numerous in the length built immediately above the Point; the winds are too searching there; this is the home of the thrift, and, on the higher stones of the wall, of the grey-green lichens which flourished best in the salty driven spume.

There they live, like strange hair of forgotten sea-spirits, relics of an age forgotten in the earth's travail.

Farther along the wall, where it turns inland, beside the green sheep-track in the furze, the grey lichens give place to orange-yellow lichens spreading flat on the surface of the stone-flakes; and here clumps of sea-thrift are seen only occasionally.

Here on the top of the wall remains some of the soil of the original bonding. It is a fibrous soil; indeed, it consists almost entirely of decaying fragments of the roots of past generations of stunted plants.

Here exist the poorest plants, which all their lives must struggle to be themselves in the place where their seeds were lodged by wind or birds.

Consider this sow-thistle which, had the wind borne it over the wall on its parachute, might have grown tall and straight, its stem and branching leaves thick with milky sap. By chance the seed fell in a crevice between two stones, and there the seedling had to find what holding it could; there it must live; there it must make its seeds; and there it must die.

Every wind sought to scour more soil from the crack, every rain washed more of its rootlets bare, but it hung on, while succeeding gusts shook it and wore away its dwarfed leaves. The entire plant was no wider than my finger-nail, no taller than my finger-joint; over the wall grew its brother, already 2ft. high.

Its tap-root, which held it to life, was fibrous and thin as cotton; the leaves, no larger than the wings of a wasp, had turned purple, the hue of last hope, desperately to absorb more of the vital sunrays. A rabbit had eaten half of the "milkydashel" in one bite.

Milkydashel, milky thistle, is the name given by village boys, who seek it in the hedgerows for their tame rabbits; its sap is white, for it is not a true thistle, but of the dandelion family.

There the poor plant had endured the winter, one of the "hopelessly unfit," waiting to put forth its yellow bloom to attract a bee to pollinate its seeds, thus to assure its immortality.

Seeing its human equivalent, what are our thoughts? Of the poor dashel I know this: there was no destitution in the seed when it was lodged there.

April 16, 1945

EVERYTHING LOOKS BRIGHTER NOW

The brilliant azure of the open sky illumines the mossy white blossoms of the pear tree just outside my workroom window.

It is a large window, running almost the entire southern length of the room. The room is bare, with walls of cream distemper; the boards are scrubbed like the deck of a wooden ship; and when I sit there at a small three-legged table – in the midst of light and air – I feel the nearest to freedom that a man can feel in this world in these times.

At night I see the stars on their westward sweep across the hemisphere, as I lie on a couch against the wall. Sometimes searchlights sweep the skies; flares burn beyond the horizon of the hill; but it is the stars which bring clarity to the mind.

During the past five years I had almost forgotten the stars; night was an occasion for pulling the black curtains across the wide window, with its 36 panes of glass each a foot square, and shutting out "reality." Now the sky is almost clear again; and the stars have meaning once more.

And as though Nature, outraged and occluded for so long, wished to make the eternal truths unmistakably plain to man, suddenly I find myself marvelling at the colours of this April month, as I sit by the open window.

Why is the blossom of the pear tree, its branches almost touching the pantiles of the roof of the woodshed below my windowsill, so white and so thick? And the colours of the bullfinch on a twig amidst the blossoms – black of head, breast of burnt red earth, and grey of back – why are they so startlingly sharp, fresh and "new?"

Is it the mental relief one feels as the patient, the crisis past, may suddenly see with an exceptional clarity the primary virtues and colours of the world?

An acquaintance recently back from visiting a friend who is a soldier, and also an artist, told me that when he suggested to his friend that he used to find relaxation from the cares of a very great military responsibility in taking an odd hour off occasionally to paint the landscape, the reply was "My men in the line cannot paint, and so I could not either."

That is what one would expect; it is a thought natural to a man of sensibility, who has transcended the "little ego" or self.

Beyond the limits of self there are thoughts or feelings which guide and rule a man, I would almost say involuntarily; as the stars sweep westward across the hemisphere set in their orbits by the immutable forces of the cosmos.

In the circumstances of a war no great art can flourish; no true artist could detach himself from it, for he too is ruled and guided by fixed forces of the spiritual world which is perceived by way of the human imagination.

I do not remember such a sky, such a clear light, such a crystalline flow and ambience of light as now, across the island from sea to sea, fills the April days as the war in Europe comes towards its end.

Were leaves of oak (coming before the ash) ever so ruddy, so bronze? And look at the little cherry-tree down the garden, planted two years ago, and now scarcely four feet high; a pyramid of massed white.

Across the valley I can see the green of the oats on the ploughed home hills; and on the skyline two partridges walking side by side. Nearer the wood a hare is feeding; his ears are floppy, he is at peace, for the breezes of the hill tell him that no enemy is near; and from where he squats, he can see all around him.

He must be five hundred yards away, but I can see one ear up and one down; or am I deceiving myself in this startlingly clear air?

Well, I had a glass once! Unused for years; it has lain there in its leather case in the chest of drawers in the next room. Here it is again – the war nearly over – and how good it looks!

Now, are those ears flopping or are they not? Magnification eight times; a clear focus; my eye did not deceive me; there is a magnifying quality in the air, in the heated air ascending without tremor or crinkle – without the mirage-effect of July and August.

The lilac is out and scenting the air; and from the bushes hiding the old draw-well there steal the first low notes of the nightingale, come from across the deserts of Africa, through the mountain passes of the Alps where hang, amidst the peaks, the tatters of a parachute, and below on the slopes, where the snow is melting, the deep blue flowers of the gentians.

April 23, 1945

REVOLUTION ON BRITAIN'S FARMS

The English countryside to-day reveals a happy scene, compared with six years ago. I speak of the fields of arable and grass of the unspoiled farmlands.

Hedges which once sprawled 10 and 15 feet high, and several yards into weedy fields, are now trim and tidy. Meadows rank with rough grasses and clumps of rushes are smooth and a uniform green with new kinds of grass mixtures.

In the arable districts of England you see farm after farm of smooth and pleasant fields, set with thin green threads of growing sugar-beet, of dark blue-green oats, paler barley and robust wheat.

Up here in Norfolk I can search in field after field of corn and hardly find a weed anywhere, except in the hedge bottoms. Machines spraying sulphuric acid, copper sulphate, and other chemicals have long since wilted the yellow charlock, shrivelled the plants of poppy, wild radish, and even the thistle. In some fields the weeds have died out altogether.

On these big farms, some of them of thousands of acres, machines do most of the work. Where years ago patient horses, led by a boy, plodded before a man guiding a horse-hoeing outfit down the green threads of growing sugar-beet, slowly to cut the thistles and other weeds with knives a few inches under the soil, now tall thin-wheeled tractors move, taking eight rows at a time.

The wide steel hoeing machine is fixed under and before the driver; he can steer to within an inch of the threadlike rows of tiny plants, cutting the roots of every weed.

Haymaking is a thing of the past on some of these great rural factories; the growing grass, stimulated by artificial fertilisers, is cut and lifted on teams of trailers, taken to the headquarters of the factory (once called the farm premises), and dried over metal trays in blasts of scorching air driven by great fans before glowing coke furnaces. The dried grass comes out in bales, green and sweet.

On some of these modern farms not a tame animal exists. Everything that is grown in the fields is sold for money; nothing is retained. In one operation the corn is cut, threshed, and taken away in lorries to the driers – big foundries like the grass-drying plants – where the extra mildew-making moisture is removed.

The harvest is over almost as soon as begun. The straw on the field is picked up by one machine and baled by another machine; and sold for paper making.

Everything is turned into cash; nothing grown for home consumption; no oats, for there are no horses; no beet-pulp is bought from the factories, for there are no bullocks to feed.

The men are mechanics; the labourers are no more. Most of the work is done at contract prices, called "taken work." The mechanics prefer it that way, as they are working directly for themselves. When they have finished their day's work they wash, change and relax.

In these modern businesses, too, the "farmer" or managing director has a good time; he shoots often four days a week in the season, often keeps a string of hunters, and is seen about in the most expensive types of sports car.

Some agriculturalists who doubted this type of farming before the war – saying it was "ruining the land, taking it all out and putting nothing back" – have now decided to farm that way in the Peace. They say that sugar-beet "tops" – the green leaves struck off when the long root is thrown into cart or lorry, sometimes by a machine – ploughed in rot down and form sufficient humus; and the aftermath of the grass-cuttings, also turned in by the plough, maintains the fertility of the land.

And why have all the worry and loss through fattening bullocks in order to tread straw into muck to grow the corn and the beet, when all the costly labour of straw-carting, muck carting and spreading can be eliminated by ploughing in "tops" and grass aftermath, and the sowing of artificial or chemical fertiliser by a machine?

Most of the big arable farmers are now planning to put down half their arable acreage to grass, and to sell dried grass as a crop; and the other half in corn and beet all mechanically sown and harvested. No sheep, no horses, no bullocks, "not a beast on the place!" No more trouble with men.

I went last March to see a farm which for years has been mechanised like that. Most of the land is light land, sandy and gravelly. In old times sheep fed-off on roots turned themselves into mutton, while "golden hoofs" compressed the land, and they manured it for the growing of the finest malting barley.

I went there when the east wind was blowing hard. I watched streams of tiny sharp flints and sand moving before the blasts, cutting the tender barley plants. In the new gateways, twenty feet wide to take the American combine-harvesters, sand was piling up before the winds. Was this the answer to the controversy, "You can't farm without muck?"

Elsewhere farmers, mindful of this ominous phrase, are experimenting with heavy disk ploughs, which turn in the straw left in swathes by the combine-harvesters. One I know disks the straw-strewn stubbles immediately behind the harvester in August, and drops mustard seed in the loose soil.

Pheasants love mustard, it gives them cover from view and they can run swiftly through it; it "draws" the birds.

The small farmer, with his 1914 horse-reaper, his life a continual worry of stack-building and threshing, of laborious digging and loading and carting – and always with the dread of the work getting on top of him, so that he may miss the timely cultivations and sowings – wonders what farming is coming to.

May 14, 1945

THE BIRD VOICE THAT IS FADING

A smallholder to whom I lend a piece of land by the river, where he grazes a pony in exchange for keeping the weeds cut, came to me with a dead bird in his hand.

It was slender and streaked in yellow, reddish brown and umber. Its head and beak revealed that it got its livelihood by picking up seeds and insects in corn and grass. Could I tell him what it was?

I was not sure; so I called the bird-boy of our family, Rikky. He didn't know either. We had several old books, with coloured plates and began a search through them. We decided that the bird was not a quail; its legs were too long; it was one of the Rail family, I thought, until a plate showed it to be a corncrake.

I had not heard or heard of a corncrake in eight years living on this North Norfolk coast. Years ago they used to be common throughout England. I have heard them in North Devon, in the misty moonlit nights of early summer, hour after hour as the ventriloquial *crake crake* of the bird's voice ran in the grassy fields before the hay was cut; a dry, slightly harsh frog-like voice seeming to come first from the side of the field by the hedge, then from the middle, and then to recede farther, only to return a moment later.

In those days, when I was out of the Army and it seemed that never again could there be another war, I used to spend a lot of time on the hills at night, often staying out until dawn, enchanted by the sense of solitude and freedom, the timelessness and tranquillity of the remote country; watching and wandering as the moon arose out of Exmoor and climbed up and across the starry sky, and to descend to the west and to grow pale with the coming of the dawn.

It was an enthralling thing, to see the hill-line hedges grow blacker, sharper, to see the stars shorn of their flashing, and, standing a thousand feet above the ocean, to know that light like a tide was flowing over the eastern rim of the earth, to bring joy to the day once more. The luminous tide filled the sky to the zenith; the sky glowed like porcelain.

The morning star arose while yet the sun was far down the curve of the earth's surface. It seemed to me like a mayfly, trailing its legs – which were the beams of light – in the dark stream of night, whose gravelly bed glinted with stars.

As the porcelain began to absorb more light, the morning star shone with a whiter, more intense glow; and when the azure of dawn lay above the moor, making the outlines of trees sharp and black, Lucifer was but a brilliant point of light. Lucifer, the lightbringer, the mythical angel whose powers of bringing clarity to life were unique; and who mistook his purpose in direct action; Lucifer vanishes as the omnipotent sun rises to shine upon the world; the life-giving sun which sees no shadows.

Yet Lucifer is the herald of the sun, and in the darkness men see hope and beauty embodied in him. Do not dismiss the mythology of the ancients as so much fairy-story stuff; they knew tyranny and suffering in wars as we do; the old poets were wise, with powers of divination that were equal to those of modern psychology. The world is not "clear" to-day; its machines have merely intensified the problem of human salvation; the very machinery which has nearly destroyed the little innocent corncrakes who make their nests and sit on their eggs, and to see them broken, in the long grasses of young summer.

May 23, 1945

SO I LEFT THEM ALONE

A low, discreet chattering outside the window of my hut drew me to the door. It was quiet on the hilltop, nearly a thousand feet above the sea.

The summer air strayed in the bright green leaves of trees; the cold dewy air of morning was already changing into the flowing clarity of an open summer sky.

The chattering came from a magpie who had suddenly spied me by the open window of the hut. I went among the small trees and saw the nest at once in a larch, six feet above my head.

In the field rows of potato plants were growing; the iron scuffler to cut the weeds stood at the top of the field, awaiting the farmer and his horse.

The magpie I knew to be a cunning bird. It was a bandit, which robbed other birds. It watched for their nests, then slipped down, its long black tail spread, to take the eggs, or the young. It worked down a hedge or through a spinney as a weasel worked underneath among the tree roots.

And judging others by itself (also a human trait), the magpie built a nest to baffle other feathered bandits. It pleached short twigs of thorns above the nest, making a canopy or roof which gave cover from view and also obstructed a direct entry. Being untrustworthy itself, the magpie did not trust others of the Crow family, which lived by robbery.

I got a ladder and climbed up and put my hand into the hole at the side. As I had imagined from the soft throaty chakkering of the parent magpie, young birds were within. They were not yet fledged; I could feel their hot naked skins. One tried to swallow my little finger. They were about a week old. I got down again.

By the door of the hut, almost hidden in the long grasses, lay an old pig trough, hewn hundreds of years ago out of a slab of rock.

The field on the hilltop was nearly a mile above the stream in the valley, and the water of the trough alone nourished the small birds of the hilltop. These were thrushes and blackbirds, hedge sparrows, wrens, robins, whitethroats, chaffinches and tomtits. All these birds enjoyed sanctuary until the pair of magpies, drawn by the cover of the plantation of ash, beech, fir, birch and hazel, came to claim the territory. Thereupon began the yearly tyranny over the nests of the small birds.

Had I been living in the hut, the magpies would never have built their nest a few feet away from it. Three years before they had chosen the same place, but not the same tree. They chose that place because the tallest pines gave them a lookout all around.

My coming put them out. They did not make the mistake again of chakkering to their young. The nestlings also ceased to speak in that small throaty mutter at the top of the larch tree. During the days that followed I never saw the old birds again. They entered the plantation at the top of the field, and slipped through the trees, from branch to branch, feeding their young in complete silence.

I deliberated whether or not I should remove the nestlings and so save the young of half the small birds in the field; but the thought had scarcely come into my head before I knew I would leave them alone.

May 28, 1945

A ROBIN PERCHED ON MY TOE

I am sitting on a little grassy terrace before a house built a thousand feet above the sea. Immediately below me the cliff slopes away steeply to the rocky bay which is reached by paths through the oak trees.

Years ago a man came here and thought it the ideal place to live. He brought chalk from France and burned it in a kiln at the edge of the rocks, thus making it into lime. He slaked the lime and mixed it with sand from the rocky shore and laboriously built a quay, where sailing ships might unlade coal and more chalk for building other houses.

It was a tricky quay to berth at; the rise and fall of the tides was rapid, the waves swept in and broke harshly, and the bottom of the sea with littered with crags fallen from the cliffs.

The quay was built not so very long ago. Men still able to do a day's work remember declaring that the "gravel" of the shore was not "sharp" enough to make hard mortar to bind the rocks which formed the quay. It was smooth, of grey shillet – a slaty substance, and soft. To-day the remains of the quay lie scattered, covered with limpets, on the shore; and young men and women walking round the coast, along the perilous narrow and winding tracks through the stunted oaks and pear trees, wild yews and ash trees, linger there to feel the timeless-ness of the elements – the safety of eternity – in the wild scenery.

For man dreams, and strives to set up the materialisation of his hopes; and Time wears them away, aided by the elements which rule as they have ruled for millions of years. The ravens croak softly over the rocky beach now as they did when William Rufus thought to make of the Forest of Exmoor the greatest deer preserve in Europe.

The buzzards wail over the cliffs and the gulls pursue them, as in those far-off days; the peregrine sweeps across the blue and falls in his shattering stoop on a rock pigeon; the hind with her "calf" lies contentedly in the shade of the oaks; the cormorant paddles and tips up and swims underwater after fish.

There are no mental problems when one is relaxed to the fair elements. I am as I was made; I am one with the spirit of rustling leaf and airborne feather, of wave and rock, of the sunlit clouds lying over distant Wales. Have men drowned in that far wrinkled width of sea that is never still, as it moves always to follow faithfully the constant orbits of the moon?

A robin came and perched on my toe-cap. He is a stranger to me.

He cocked his head and regarded me with a beady eye before flitting off to seek crumbs from the tablecloth which an hour or two ago was shaken on the lawn.

The lawn? No mower has passed over this close mat of grasses for many a year. Yet the turf is fine and level. If you sit here as the sun is dropping towards the west, and remain still when two ears and a large brown eye prospecting regard you for some moments, you will see first one rabbit, then another rabbit, and perhaps a third and fourth, suddenly hop over the edge, a few feet away, and begin to pull and pare the grasses – the daily half-inch of growth – with their teeth.

An old bull mastiff lies under the veranda, but they do not heed him; he is the local patriarch of four footed things, and his presence serves only to reassure the rabbits that the low shaggy Scots terrier with the melancholy eyes is not about. For when John (as his master calls him) lies there, the terrier is usually round at the back, near the kitchen door.

Not that the rabbits mind the squat black dog who sometimes lets out a yelp and runs them by scent among the ferns and the wild rhododendrons; for Hamish (as the terrier is called) invariably "hunts heel," that is runs by scent in the direction from which the rabbit has come.

Hamish is a melancholy beast; he has to find his own amusements in this remote place, for if taken for a walk Hamish, I am told, always gets lost; and whenever he meets another dog he acts as *agent provocateur*, growls and bristles only to lie on his back with four paws up when a fight is imminent, to be rescued by the idealistic bull mastiff.

There is Hamish peering round the corner. He watches me with genial but bleary eyes before coming to squat by my foot, which he has come to know as an obliging scratching post. He groans with pleasure; but look! two ears are projecting over the edge of the lawn, with a still brown eye. The lawn-mowers have arrived.

For a while Hamish vacillates between the pleasure of being scratched (indistinguishable from being spurned by my toe-cap) and the call of his sporting 11-year-old blood. Blood will tell, and, hoarsely barking, Hamish sets out on a hunt towards the West, while the rabbit lollops away into the East.

June 4, 1945

Margaret, Rikky, Robbie and John on the saltmarshes

THIS SPARROW SINGS AND FIGHTS

I have read somewhere in Richard Jefferies that the colours from the wings of sparrows faded long ago. That finest of English country writers may have got the idea from Darwin; anyway, it is a theory; for no one can be sure. But I think it is probable.

The town sparrow is a finch with a hard shrill, unmusical voice. He is quarrelsome, untidy, and his habits have probably degenerated. That is to say, no other finches behave as the town sparrow behaves.

None makes those untidy, straggling nests of dried grass, straw, lengths of rag, fragments of paper, old bootlaces, string, and other bits of rubbish loosely put together.

The cock sparrow can sing, in a way, if it can be called singing. He sits on a gutter, or in a smoke-grimed tree, and chirps. He will flutter away to join in a quarrel as soon as sing. How came he to degenerate like this? How came the rosy-faced countryman to become, after a generation or two, a pale-faced, repressed human being seen too frequently in the poorer parts of any large town at the beginning of this century?

It does not take long for rosy cheeks to fade in a sunless street of houses and factories. Perhaps it did not take long for the colours to fade from the wings of that immigrant street-finch called the sparrow. Were colours needed when living was easy in streets where for centuries horses were passing and repassing every day? For colours on wings have a purpose in nature; and they are maintained by fidelity to that purpose, or spiritual impulse.

Once the finch gets into slack habits, when living is easy, when there is little need to attract or to win a mate by display of coat or song, once the spiritual impulse slackens the whole nature and appearance of the bird slackens, too.

The other day I trimmed an overgrown hedge on a Devon hilltop and, by good fortune, paused with the steel slasher in time to see a chaffinch's nest in the little fork of a thorn tree in the hedge. There were no eggs in it; obviously it had been made for a second brood. It was not built with the extreme care shown by a chaffinch in April; it was not deep like one of those moulded mossy nests which are perfect in symmetry and proportion. But the authentic care and craftsmanship was there; the instinctive craftmanship which had not been corrupted by easy pickings in an urban street where the leaves of trees, at least during the early part of this century, were grimed and

48

sick with soot and sulphur fumes of an industrial civilisation, stifling in more ways than one.

The chaffinch's nest was a beautiful thing to behold: every piece of moss and lichen placed with care and pleached into place, and the passionate breast of the bird pressing as it turned, again and again, in its beak horsehair or feather, lambs' wool or occasional fine grass, to weave and press the nest into the cavity of its shape.

While the hen-bird was building the cock-bird watched and, mounted on a spray of an ash tree, sang to her. His breast was copper-coloured, and the crown of his head was blue-grey. His eye was bright and full; there was no low street-cunning in it. Yet in other respects he was not so different in build from his cousin in the towns, whose life had become unbalanced by the adoption of an environment which did not do justice to his evolutionary purpose. Perhaps when towns have their green belts, and their wider streets, and their rosy checks again, the colours of the sparrows' wings will return under the blue skies which helped to make them.

June 20, 1945

IN A VILLAGE THAT CHANGED

On Midsummer Eve I left the little inn built on the rock, where for over thirty years I had known most of the faces that sat round the table after the day's work, and started to walk up the hill to my abode among the trees.

It was two minutes after closing time; 10.30 p.m. D.S.T.; yet it was scarcely owl-light. The white owl still brooded inside the church tower. Beyond the Rectory trees the sunset was gleaming on the Atlantic.

What was the hurry? Without premeditation, we sat on the step of the inn and talked of the changes come over the world since the days when I had first known the village; when beer was twopence a pint, cider a penny, and cottages could be rented for a shilling a week. In those days men of a neighbouring village were still regarded as half-enemies. Champion wrestlers were living whose shins were scarred with old kicks of the iron-capped "wrestling" boots.

Between the ending of the Boer War and August 1914 village champions, with their followers, used to meet on waste ground between villages and hold kicking matches. Shaven polls were the thing, lest your opponent get a grip on your hair. You could grip him where you could, above the big leather belt he wore – with its brass buckle often felt by disobedient children.

The man who could stand the pain of savage hacking and the loss of blood longest was the champion.

I first came to the village when the last of the matches had been held; but hostility between villages still echoed in various remarks. It was no longer active; and the cause was scientific, technical: to wit, in the adaptation of the wheel.

The real widening of the human consciousness came with the motorcar. I remember how the white-washed cottage walls were pink from the dust raised off the iron-stone roads; several dogs being run over, before a generation was born wheel-conscious. I recall the first flying-boats coming off the Atlantic and passing over the village, and the terror of the blacksmith's hens, which ran squawking into the darkness of his forge, away from the monstrous great hawks.

That was after the first World War when a cottage in the village sold for £40, to be done up and to be let furnished a few years later at £20 a week in August. These and other details came to my mind as I sat with others outside the Rock Inn on a midsummer night.

What a change in the village mentality since those early days! I can testify that there is a wider understanding of others and with it less personal rancour.

At 11 o'clock most of them went "oomwards," for mangold hoeing was hard work by day and also the hay was fit to be cut. Two acquaintances of the seashore walked with me towards the hilltop trees. We crossed a field, and heavy drops of rain beginning to fall, we sought shelter under a corrugated iron shelter for haystacks.

Lying on a cut shelf of last year's hay, we watched the summer lightning playing silently across the sky in great sudden flaring luminous sheets, in soundless glows revealing the hedgerow trees as though set in stone. No roll of thunder; all in complete silence, save for the lisp of wind in the leaves and the long grasses of the meadow.

So midnight came and passed, and one o'clock, then two o'clock, and we sat there, talking in quiet voices, while the moths fluttered in the twilit spaces of the shelter, and far off on the hill a nightjar churred and reeled to the moon.

I had first known this magic of Devon thirty-one years ago, when the little low jingles, drawn by moorland ponies, were the only means of transport between the villages and the market town; I had lived through two wars and had come to think that the old scenes were spoiled for evermore; and yet, how wrong I was.

Here it all was, just as before – England everlasting.

June 28, 1945

THE ROBIN THAT STAYED UP LATE

Standing at twilight on the steps of a caravan which for four years of war had sheltered the wife and young family of a soldier, I noticed a small movement in a flower bed.

It was nearly midnight by Double Summer Time. The reeling song of the nightjar came with the rising of the moon out of the moorland vapours; moths were fluttering in the long grasses.

It was time to go to bed, after a long day on the sands and among the rocks after crabs and lobsters.

"There's a rat down there," I said. "Do you see the slow, stealthy movement? I wonder what it is eating." "Oh, that's Ruddock, our tame robin," said my friend.

The field where the caravan stood was nearly a mile from the village, and half a mile from the nearest water. There was an old pig-feeding trough near the hedge, chipped from a slab of stone centuries ago, holding about a gallon of water.

All the small birds in twenty acres knew it, and came there to sip and bathe.

My friend first met her friendly robin when in 1940 she was teaching herself to make a garden. He flew to watch her as she was laboriously cutting tough squares of grass – tough, thick clumps of cocksfoot grass – to make heaps to rot down into compost. The robin came for worms and insects, after the habit of its kind.

My friend had a determined character, and stuck at her job of making a garden in the wilderness. She was a book-gardener, with no experience of growing vegetables, flowers, and fruit. But she did not tire of her task, and what to others appeared to be a lonely life, swept by winds and ocean rains in winter and beset by roof-warping heats in the summer sun, was to her a natural existence that brought peace of mind in the temporary failure of civilisation.

She worked steadily, during the anxieties of the African desert fighting and the anguish of all the peoples of the earth – one of millions of women maintained by faith. In her small "parcel" of land she planted fruit trees and flowering shrubs; she set out beds of strawberries and raspberries, with potatoes, onions, greenstuffs for salads, and winter cabbages.

In all this work Ruddock, the robin, was her constant working companion. From perching on the handle of spade and fork, he dared to fly direct to her shoulder, watching for wireworm or grub or worm to be turned up. Sometimes he sang a few bars of a song. In a world full of mistrust there was trust between this small bird and the young mother and her children.

In spring Ruddock got a mate, and made a nest in the bank, coming into the caravan for food for his mate and fledgelings. Usually the pair raised a second brood, after which he lived alone for the rest of the season.

The gardener was busy with two children during the day, with mending and making clothes, and all the other jobs of running a home, which was maintained by the best standards of neatness and cleanliness, for the sake of morale or self-discipline. The robin, too, had these high standards by instinct; he was regular in his habits, he bathed twice a day, he sang in praise of life after his work, and came to see his friend.

Ruddock learned to be a late bird. Since the gardener often worked late into the summer evenings, he got out of the habit of going to roost when the other day-birds became silent and unseen. Long after sunset he stayed by the flower beds, watching as the hoe struck at weed of dock and groundsell, at sow-thistle and spurrey.

He became almost diurnal beside his human companion; and even when she was not working on hands and knees on the beds, he worked by himself, examining the clods and granules of earth out of long habit. Born probably in the first year of the war, he was by the ending of the German war an old bird, perhaps the equivalent of 60 or 70 human years. This last spring Ruddock did not have a mate, but passed his days in and around the caravan, roosting in an Austrian pine in the little triangular spinney.

And there he was, pottering by himself in a flower-bed near to midnight while the moon, distended and pink-yellow, like a great salmon-egg washed in the vapours above the distant estuary, was rising over the primeval moor. I was about to say good-night, and go to my hut among the trees in the lower corner of the field, when the dark shape of a wood owl suddenly fluttered over the hedge and glided down to the small lawn between caravan and flower beds. The vulnerability of this curiously tame little robin to an owl's talons in the dim light had been in my mind a moment before, with a thought of what I would do should one suddenly appear; so I was not surprised. Before I could think again I found myself uttering a shout and leaping off the steps, my arms outspread, a growling noise coming from my throat.

Shocked by the apparition, the owl swept up and beat abruptly away; the robin uttered stittering cries of anger and fear, and vanished; while in the darkness came the rising, falling, reeling song of the nightjar, and the flashes of the lighthouses on the rocks of the Atlantic coast.

July 4, 1945

WHAT SHALL I DO ABOUT HARVEST?

There is no wind over the rustling cornfields; it is heated air in motion. There is no refreshment in the wafts of heated air upon which the first thistledown of the year is floating.

Two days ago I motored up to the North Norfolk coast from Southern England, where I had been to collect parts of a milking machine. I drove an open-bodied "Silver Eagle" car – faithful companion of nearly 15 years. Once it was what was called, in those pre-war days, a sports model.

Every few miles, the harvest maturity of the corn was changing. Barley was bleaching out in Sussex while it was yet yellow in Surrey, and on the same day yellow-green in Hertfordshire and, coming to Norfolk, still green. And what yields! I'll say it is the best barley crop in England since the glut-year of 1938 which met a trade depressed by over 100 per cent almost overnight . . . the year of Munich, when much of the Central European crop was bought up hastily by British money. The barley harvest this year should solve the beer problem from Michaelmas onwards.

What are my thoughts, as a farmer facing his seventh war-time harvest? Are they of any value, as an indication of what other farmers are thinking and feeling? They may be; for if my seven years of farming have taught me anything, it is that I am limited by nature even as they are; that intellectual ideas are one thing and that "real life" is another.

Which means, I suppose, that ideas change but human nature remains pinned to and limited by its fundamental instincts and feelings.

As a man, as a farmer, I am a little tired. Before the war a farmer used to lie abed at night wondering if he would be able to sell what he had grown. During the war he lay abed wondering if he would be able to get his crops sown in time, and then, if he could get them off in time. Before the war labour was certain, but markets were problematical; during the war markets were certain, but labour was the problem. Now the farmer wonders if farming will be as before the war; or will the problems of labour and markets be balanced? Is it possible, under a free system?

Meanwhile, harvest is imminent, and its severe problems. It has already begun in the South. Where am I to get enough men to bring in my hundred acres of corn? Will Italian prisoners be available?

Will they work as they did on other jobs in the past? On our farm in the past we found that four Eyeties did almost as much work in a day as one British labourer, and they did it on approximately eight times the protein intake, augmented by various small birds, rabbits, hares, moorfowl and game they snared and cooked.

Farming is one long battle, most of it hidden behind the farmer's eyes. When I began I said that nothing would stop me. "You'll larn," said an old man to me in my first year. "Not your way," I said. "You who believe that the father of a mushroom is a stallion." "Yer'll larn," he repeated, and the cry was echoed from a distant tree, where some Norfolk rooks were waiting for me to go away from the corn I had just sown. And in eight years, yes, I think I have learned.

I've learned tolerance. I've learned to submit to what I cannot alter: human nature. Conrad wrote that to learn to submit was one of the fundamental lessons of life. I wonder, is it the same as being defeated? To learn that aspiration and the human will-power are not irresistible, that human courage is expendable? The ploughshare, once bright, rusts in the corner of the harvest field. Does it matter?

July 24, 1945

KNIVES AND WEEDS

In the summer weather the sluggish river rose slowly, with the great growth of green water-weeds. As the farmer walked along by the meadow he saw the rise of water from several angles.

As a bullock grazier, the water would rise also in the meadows and check the growth of the good grasses.

As a fly-fisherman, he knew the river-weeds would give cover to the few trout which otherwise in a bare river-bed would be easy prey for herons and the numerous village poachers with their small barbed tridents on the end of long poles.

As a naturalist, he noted the white flowers of the water crowsfoot, the emerald green sprays of the starwort, the darker green of Canadian pondweed – that weed which to English rivers was as the rabbit in Australia.

He saw the water-birds sporting on the calm, slow-moving stretches; the courtships and rivalries of moorhens and dabchicks; he heard the cries of summer sandpipers by the brimming river's edge, and saw the snipe zigzagging in flight over the lush meadows.

On two of the far meadows wheat was standing, nearly ripe for the cutter. Would the water brim into the "lows," causing tractor and reaping machine to get bogged down? The weeds should be cut at once. He telephoned to the Catchment Board engineer, who said all three men should be put on the job at once.

In the old days of the pre-war this river was regarded solely as a drain. The ideal of the river men was to leave not one water weed growing out of its bed. And the river must always be widened, to clear the mud which rose higher every year. In still older days, before the first German war, before the Catchment Board was formed, the river was free of mud. It was no uncommon thing to see from the old brick bridge a hundred trout rings in the river at once as the fish rose for the evening.

But with the placing of culverts and pipes to drain the roads, with their bitumenised surfaces, rain water got quickly into the river; and with the rain water, mud, oil, to silt the sandy bed.

After every rainy day the mud lay thicker; and warmed by the summer sun, the mud gave off bubbles of carbon dioxide, which meant that the living oxygen in the water, by which both fish and delicate ephemeral water-flies lived, was absorbed by the black decay. The river was dying.

When the farmer first went there, from the pure living streams of the West Country, he vowed to purify the stream, by words both written and spoken, and by his own actions. Very soon he found obstruction to this idea.

The willow slips he planted on his own river bank, to grow into trees to be pollarded and give shade to the water and beauty to the valley, were pulled out and cut down. He planted a thousand one long spring day and evening; less than a hundred survived.

To experiment with waterflows, he put elmboards diagonally across half the river, to shift some of the mud downstream and so out under the tide doors. Out they come!

He tried to point out that the wider the river bed was made, the slower would be the flow, and the slower the flow, the greater the deposit of silt, the higher the river bed.

Make the water shift the silt, he said: let the stream throw it about, let boards create turbulence, whirl the water about. No good. The stream, like so many in England, must die. It was the age of frustration.

But with the war came a change. Others grew interested in the possibilities of fly-fishing. It was said that a race of unique hybrid trout lived in the river; a cross between native brown and imported rainbow from California.

A farmer more practical than our literary farmer saw at once how the question of pollution should be tackled. The milk of cows drinking from the river was affected!

Old habits die hard. Seeing the water brimming 2ft. higher by the excessive weed growth, our farmer telephoned the authorities. The authorities acted immediately, saying the weeds would be cut that very day. A telegram to the river-men was sent off. The river-men, who lived in the village, were dismayed; for the only knives owned by the Board to cut the weeds with were 20 miles away!

There was but one other set of chain-knives they knew of, and they belonged to Farmer W., and Farmer W. would not have the weeds cut! Even when it was explained to them that it was Farmer W. who had telephoned for the cutting, the three river-men demurred: Farmer W. wouldn't have them weeds cut! So we dursant ask him for the loan of his knives. He'll mob us if we do.

So Farmer W. took his chain-knives to them, as a loan. Even so, there was demur. There was a catch in it somewhere!

Funny fellow, Farmer W.; nobody can make him out; first he talks for years about not cutting the weeds, and now he says they ought to be cut. What can you make of that, 'bor? It's a rum 'un!

July 30, 1945

FISHING WITH A BAMBOO POLE

When the moon is new, and again when it is full, the tides lapse farthest from the rocks and return swiftly to the highest lines of jetsam on the sands.

Then is the time to take the long bamboo stick from the corner of the room, to beat out the rusty iron hook lashed to its end so that the tip of the hook is sharp, to put on old clothes and nailed boots, and with bag slung over shoulder and net in hand, go down the shore where the immemorial lobster and crab holes are exposed by the low tide.

Sometimes you wade to your waist in water made darker by marine litter and a tangle of brown thong weeds; at other times you kneel with your bent toe-caps in a thin plash of sun-glittering salt.

But you must be swift, for the tide waits for no man.

Crabs usually seek the deep horizontal holes as cover while they are changing their shells. When you probe with your slender gaff and a crab is there, you may recognise him because he nips the iron and pulls it towards him. A lobster, on the other hand (or claw), pushes it away.

Sometimes you may tell when a lobster has come to take up his home in the hole in the rock by the way he has cleaned it out. The still pool of low tide may be a little coloured where he has swept with propulsive motions of his tail. Bits of seaweed and other wrack may be lying in the diffused water outside the hole.

Seeing the hook approaching, the lobster moves rapidly, thrusting it away with his great blue claws. If he is hooked by a claw, he sheds the claw at once; he does not wait to be pulled out by it. He will dodge the quarter-inch curve of iron, moving with a surprising rapidity, using his water-propelling apparatus.

If you get him out of the hole and the pool beyond the narrow cleft of rocks is deep, you have to be quick to sweep his bulk into and against your net; for he shoots away and hides instantly against the blue-green dimness of the uneven sea-bed.

The bite of a conger eel is worse than his bark. He is a fearsome thing to encounter for the first time. He will fight you. Off this coast of which I write – the Atlantic seaboard – a conger eel of 110lb. has been taken on a steel hook baited by fresh herring. A conger will as a rule eat only live fish and many a hook two inches wide across the sneck has been pulled out straight when a fisherman standing on the rocks has been hauling on his hempen line with a breaking strain of 300lb.

You have to know what you are about when you haul a conger eel into your boat off the bar. Anyway you should not be on the bar by yourself unless you have known it since boyhood: and even then, you have to watch for the sudden swell which might arise, in the calmest day, from the ocean.

One moment you are stable in a fathom of water and the next rocking in two fathoms, and the third moment your boat touches swirling sand and you are out of it, among the bass flashing past in the boil of breakers, and thinking that Shelley's fate is now your own.

A conger eel drawn into a boat is an unpredictable thing. It has immense power; it can writhe and strike irresistibly; it should never be drawn over the gunwale unstunned. This 110lb. conger I speak of was not taken in a 16ft. fishing boat with one lugsail: I doubt if they could have managed it, for no blows of wooden mallet on head and tail against the fragile gunwale could have quieted that terrific power. It must have been taken from a small trawler.

August 20, 1945

A MIRACLE ON THE BEACH

After eight years of more or less continuous work, most of it uphill, I have taken a holiday.

I have been playing on one of the beaches of England which for nearly six years have been closed or otherwise maltreated. And, moreover, I have made the discovery, of much relief to one who thought he was growing old – that the virtues of sun, air and water are pristine and everlasting.

The miracle of conversion was simple. I took off my clothes and very soon the salt sea and candent sun, the blue-stained air told me that my prevalent thoughts during the war were not permanent as I had mournfully come to believe.

What is left of the old world? I used to think to myself behind the black-out curtains of my farmhouse. By day the air vibrated and the very sky seemed to be trundling round the sun, as though a bearing of the earth were broken, and our lives, I thought, are broken.

After half an hour in the elements I was back again in the knowledge that the harmony of life was still to be found in the elements of sun and air and sea. I had no age, life was a buoyancy outside time.

For years I had been thinking that the joys of my youth were gone for ever. Though I live in the country I spend most of my days indoors, writing, or at the telephone, or in the workshop, and so feel, often acutely, all the feelings of a frustrating city life.

Work on the farm is not what many imagine it to be; the farmer rarely sees the view; his mind is engaged, cut off from free enjoyment of the elements.

I made a friend with another familiar of the elements. His name was "Tojo." "Tojo" had a wide grin; a slow husky voice; a brown body. He was seven years old; he climbed trees with his toes, he taught me a fast game of throwing one another over on the soft sand by catching the running heel.

It was a tough and rough game when played with a dozen children, but they soon learned to fall softly on the sands, to yield themselves in falling, and so it was all fun. Skilful, too; a flick of the wrist, and your victim turns half a somersault.

"Tojo" and I worked together in the treetops of my field, where many pines were planted. They were growing too tall, and needed topping if they were to remain shields against the driving Atlantic winds. The trees were so close together that one could step from tree to tree, with a sharp

Norwegian saw severing a top two to three inches thick.

"Tojo's" job was to hang on to an obstinate unfallen top and slide down with it to the base of the tree, and then drag it to the site of the bonfire in the middle of the field. His chest stuck out like a 4½-gallon barrel, his bare feet with splayed toes dug into the soil of the field. "Tojo" worked with an earnestness which I had to check, for after all he was only seven.

Near the bonfire was his Sten gun on a home-made tripod; and his parachute harness, also home-made. And who told "Tojo" that I was a wizard? He really thought I became an owl at night and sometimes a salmon swimming round the rocks of the headland.

Whether this is old news or not, you must hear about our victory bonfire. Twenty children came to it, drawn like moths to the flame. The hilltop had a view of Dartmoor and Exmoor and the lighthouses of the Atlantic coast were flashing over the western ocean.

There was a barrel of bitumen on the top of the beacon and a lot of old sump-oil on the thorns and fir branches. Flames roared up, sparks flew and drifted. One of the seven mothers of the twenty children had with great consideration brought a bottle of Jamaican rum.

When the bottle was empty we thought all England must be seeing our fire. Next morning we cooked breakfast by its embers at the edge; for the beacon was still alight. And the south wind was singing in the tree-tops where gossamers were shining.

September 6, 1945

AN HOUR ON THE CLIFF

The waves were pounding below the headland. Before me was a vast open bowl, in which hundreds of gulls were soaring, diving, side-slipping, and rising on motionless out-held wings.

The bowl was enclosed by sheer cliffs on two-thirds of its sides; it was a broken bowl on the north-west, and the long ragged Atlantic waves were coming in at the break.

The prevailing winds of the south-west had leapt over the depression, and poured into the Hole, as the bowl-like break in the land was locally called. The violent sea-winds had whipped and scoured away the very subsoil on the exposed places of the headland, but in the depression was shelter, where things might remain.

The air in the Hole was never still. When the south-west blew, a hundred currents met and clashed, spun and eddied and rebuffeted against the face of the precipice. The Hole was filled with invisible rocks of air tumbling, cascading, and heaving in the great circular hall of the winds; and the gulls and jackdaws played and amused themselves, falling and diving, side-slipping, shooting up vertically, twirling and half-rolling, muttering, croaking, and uttering wild wailing cries.

It was as I had known it in boyhood, in early youth before "the sky had turned to brass" above the Somme battlefields, after that war and before and during another war; during 30 years in which the mental war which is the reality of physical warfare was seldom away from my consciousness.

"It won't be the same ever again!" – how many times during my life had I said that to myself? It meant, of course, that I had changed; that cares, thoughts, anxieties, frustrations inherent in the so-called civilised world had changed me. But this time, surely, it would be different. Who could think of "Nature" when the entire human world was suffering so deeply?

Mankind was mastered by the machine; and more particularly, lesser machines had descended upon this coast; it had been used for battle practice. I felt I had outgrown the place; that I would meet only my own ghost if I went back.

That was merely an illusion of fatigue. On the headland were a few craters of small bombs or shells; bullet rips and tears in the turf; a few slit trenches, burst sandbags and rusty iron stakes and wire.

Soon the salt would gnaw away the iron in a few seasons, and infiltrate it into its native rock again. Jute of sandbag would rot and decay and nourish the thrift. Nothing was lost. It was the same air, sun, water; the seals were below in the waves as before, and the gulls were sitting on their nests in the ledges of the precipice face – looking no larger than white dew-drops across the vast width of the Hole.

Over the Atlantic the galleon-clouds were moving in, travellers from the Azores, from Labrador. How then was life essentially changed? And where was the ghost of myself, of my "lost innocence?" I was the same person as the boy who had come here all those years ago, but with this difference – I was the richer in friendship because now I knew what then had been unknown.

Before I had been sitting an hour among the flowers of the sea-thrift, I knew that the simple and fundamental truths of life were unaltered by experience. But I knew also this: that the truth of life is not apparent when a man is tired or stale.

For however sophisticated or disillusioned a man may think himself to be, he is, and always will be, an elemental creature: made out of the elements, maintained and restored by the elements. At least, that is true for me, since I am an ordinary man, composed of normal hopes and fears, and I think it is true for you also.

September 18, 1945

I HAVE SOLD MY NORFOLK FARM

Into the calm blue sky of St. Martin's Little Summer the smoke of an ancient 15-ton traction engine drifts slowly. So still and gold-hazy is the air that when I get up from my office stool I can hear the far-away chuffs of the steam in the engine; and sometimes a dragging, slower noise, followed by the engine racing, tells me that some of the sheaves are going into the threshing drum uncut.

Italians in brown uniforms are on the corn-stack, forking the sheaves to the old man with the knife tied to his wrist, who slashes the binder twine, while below him on the box, another man with steel-tips to his fingers feeds the endless broken waves of stalks into the roaring drum.

I know, as I return to the high yellow stool, that the old man with the knife – the bond-cutter, as they call him – is trying to slash the string of three sheaves every two seconds of time; he is eighty years old; he misses a sheaf now and then. This sheaf goes around the drum uncut, and acts as a brake on the whirling metal cylinder; and that is when I hear the engine stutter a moment.

I know it all; I can see it clearly as I sit here on one side of the double-desk, an old corn-merchant's desk where clerks in Dickens's time were sitting, shooting ink from their quill pens. I can see it more clearly than if I were there sweating and lifting sheaves, two and three at a time from the pressed mass of the flat corn-stack.

I have done that and scores of other farming jobs with every nerve and sense of my body; and those nerves and senses are surcharged and, as it were, crying out to express all that has been felt and known and suffered in the past eight years in the only way that I can express myself: through the imagination.

I have been well aware during my farming life that to be a man of action requires one kind of rhythm; and to be a writer needs a quicker, sharper rhythm. You cannot apply the quicker rhythm of the wit to the slower rhythm of the working body. If you are an artist of self-compulsive power you may tend to expect others to share your own sharp views and feelings; and these do not go with bodily labour.

For eight years I have compromised; and now, this Michaelmas, I am going to do what I want to do more than anything else on earth – to write books and plays out of my physical experiences.

So in a day or two I shall not feel too keenly that I am a failure when I go with the auctioneer, with notebook and pencil, and make a list of cows, bullocks, calves, horses, geese, ducks and hens, with their wooden houses; the circular saw and the pigs' troughs, the buried paraffin tank, wagons, water-carts, harrows, seed-drills, trainers and corn-sacks – all the "live and dead stock" of a farm being sold at the change of the farming year, Old Michaelmas Day.

There will be the printed notices and bills by the wayside, and on the day itself, lines of cars parked by the hedge – old iron merchants with their trailers, cattle dealers with their "floats," farmers in search of useful implements – all come there, with the exception of the curious, to increase their substance.

Someone is going to have a farm which in eight years has been raised from a state of near-dereliction to an official classification A.

A queen wasp strays in at the open door, flying briskly in the October sun; a tortoiseshell butterfly flaps at the window pane. Soon wasp and butterfly will be sleeping torpidly up in the rafters of this little barn which, a year or two back, was rebuilt with materials left over from the rebuilding of the farm cottages.

The last of the tomatoes ripen on the window-sill, and the tomtits in the garden have forsaken the empty down-hanging heads of the sunflowers I grew there this year. The harvest of black and grey seeds was not gathered: the tomtits and the greenfinches had what was intended for parrot food this year.

It did not worry me; I was more interested in watching the birds. Last season, on many occasions, I ran out and shouted at them to depart; they were ruining a crop of the farmer, which would send one of his sons to school for a term.

The men who have been working for me, what would become of them? Would I have to give them notice? It had been worrying me, that I was deserting them; but now I may leave with a clear mind and heart, for the new farmer wants them to work on the farm as before.

So au revoir to farming this Michaelmas! No, it is not goodbye; one has felt and known and suffered too much in the past to say that.

The swallows fly south, over the deserts of North Africa; but they return again.

October 10, 1945

A BUTTERFLY OVER THE SEA

Along the level brown length of the shingle bank grey waves of the North Sea were breaking diagonally. It was evening, and the small boy Rikky and I had the beach to ourselves.

Behind us, on reclaimed land, under the sea wall, stood the hut encampment of Italian prisoners. There, a minute or so before, we had left Antonio and the others who all day had been working on the farm.

On journeys to and from the camp he rode with them in the small box-body fitted to the Silver Eagle, now fifteen years in service to our family. How many times have we bounded swiftly up the hills of Exmoor, crossed England from west to east, carried pigs from Stiffkey to Norwich market in the trailer, and fetched back calves to the farm?

What a story the old Silver Eagle, with its worn fabric body, travelling nearly 200,000 miles, could tell. Once it ran from Islay in the Hebrides to Barnstaple in Devon in a day and a night, 600 miles down the western flank of Britain.

Here on the shingle ridge, where in summer tern and dotterel fly, there is simplification for human life in the elements: the sea, the monotone of brown pebbles, the sky joining with the horizon. Behind, in a haze of stillness, extends a low landscape of stubble and ploughland.

We are alone with the elements . . . but stay, as we walk down to the slanting slash and break of waves of the sand-drawn slope of shore, we see an R.A.F. pilot and his girl, fishing.

We have never seen them before; yet it seems natural that the girl should greet us with a smile as we approach. This is the sea coast of England; the barbed-wire has been dragged away; the mines have been lifted. The unnumbered smile of ocean of Æschylus is the mood of this happy girl with her lover; there are no more thoughts of bomber crews falling in a salt, estranging sea.

May we look in the canvas bag? There is a codling, and a flatfish; fish are actually caught off this shore!

Rikky and I came down here declaring that whatever the weather, we would swim, perhaps for the last time on this coast. But the waves are barbarous and abrupt, sucking short at the shingle; the sun is small, wan, bisected by cloud, without heat, almost without light. Such are the sunsets of this coast, rarely flamboyant as in the West Country.

Far away in Devon this sun is flaring out the day in fire which fills the sky and turns the rocky headland purple. "Rikky, every man and woman on this earth sees a different sunset."

The small boy thinks this out. "Just as every man and woman sees a different world; and strives for a different justice." But he is staring at something in the sky.

An offshore wind moves over the level top of the shingle bank, eddying invisibly about the concave wet slope of the receding tide. Above in the dulling sky a butterfly is fluttering, borne eastwards on the wind, which blows aslant the line of the shore, stroking the white flashes of the waves.

The butterfly, which may be a tortoiseshell, strives to fly along the line of the land; but the wind carries it out over the grey sea.

The fluttering dark speck rises higher, and we stand to watch it, hoping it will be able to turn inland again and find a shed or roof where it may fold its wings flat together and sleep during the coming rains and frosts.

But it is already lost. Can that tiny engine, fuelled by honey stored in its muscles, carry the frayed sails across the sea to Holland, or maybe Denmark, or even Norway?

A tiny fragment of summer is being blown away, to become again phosphate, carbon, and salts in the sea.

"Is that a sad thought, Rikky?" The boy shakes his head. "There will be other butterflies, won't there?"

The sun has faltered and gone. The youthful bomber pilot, with his memories of lost friends but with love by his side, trudges up the shingle to his motorcycle standing by the lane.

It is time for us to go, too: crank up the engine and fill the cylinders of the Silver Eagle with gas; switch on ignition; a flick of the wrist starts the engine to rumble through the worn silencer.

Small children growing up to be young men; season after season of corn turning to summer's gold, butterflies, birds, trees, faces of friends, all, all drifting down the stream of Time which some men dread as death.

An owl cries across the stubble, partridges have ceased to call in the dusk.

October 16, 1945

BUYING A HOUSE IN THREE MINUTES

Oh what a time we're having, I say
Oh what a time we're having!

Do you remember marching to the tune of that plainsong, the words of both verse and chorus being of the same monotony, in keeping with the life of the soldier? Just now we are singing it as we travel, load after load, in the trailer behind the old Silver Eagle, between Norfolk and Suffolk.

Sometimes we pass a farmcart on the roads lined with sugar-beet heaps, and wave a greeting to the carter drawing his furniture from one cottage to another. For this is the time of change; the new farming year ends and another starts; the new man enters his holding and the old man fades away. The sere leaves flutter down from the trees, while the new buds form on the twigs.

What fun it all is, in retrospect. When we sit back and laugh at our foolish "flaps" and needless worries. There was the corn to be threshed out; we had no men; Italian prisoners might come, might not.

In five days the auction sale was to be held; and instead of threshing we should be getting out the hundreds of items – drills, harrows, hurdles, harness, carts, tractor spares, rolls of sheep netting, beehives, incubators, stack-cloths, ladders, and a score of other things heavy and light. And we had to cut up 20 tons of logs from our wood-piles on the circular saw, and take them down into Suffolk, while yet the saw and the tractor and the big trailer were ours.

After the auction sale, it would be too late. So Rikky and I, clad in overalls, got to work. John came home from school to help. What a job, piling 20 tons of seasoned logs.

The rasp of the circular saw rang day after day in the valley; the corn came down the steep hill in the lorry.

In flying helmets and coats, the two boys and I started South, arriving at the new home 60 miles away and unloading; then after tea, starting back, usually in darkness.

We got home about 10 p.m. and the next day we did it all over again, loading sacks of potatoes and onions, boxes of apples, planks of wood, corner cupboards, and baskets filled with tools.

But the 20 tons of logs, how would we get them shifted? Then we found a driver who came over and took six tons away, stacked almost as neatly in his lorry as bees build their honey-cells in the comb. That was a weight off the mind!

But the books to be packed, and the hundredweights of manuscripts! For a while I contemplated sending the entire lot to salvage, or to the flames. Windows to be taken out, to remove the furniture from the bedrooms! Fortunately the frames were put in years ago with brass screws set in grease, so that will not take long.

Then there are the hams on the beam, dark with pickling in black treacle and frilled with green penicillin; a fishing net, bundles of tobacco leaves (which the Customs officials are welcome to smoke if they can survive the first few puffs), heavy iron cauldrons and fire-dogs and kettles from the open hearths; and a mighty lot of sawn yew-wood which we brought up from Devon years ago, from trees felled in 1936, which had been planted 900 years before, for bow-wood, by the knight who carried William the Conqueror's shield at Hastings.

These splendid planks, some nearly 3ft. wide, salmon-pink, heavy and hard to work, are probably unique in England. One day they may be tables and perhaps a stairway in a house. However, we will not say too much about that; for this Devon yew-wood was intended for a staircase in a new house on the Norfolk hill; and where is that dream now?

The new house pleases us all. It was bought after three minutes' rapid run-over; seven bedrooms, oak-slab floors, lattice windows, open hearths, water laid on and electric light, built 300 years ago of oak, brick and plaster, dry and sound, a wonderful place for children's hide-and-seek, with its queer passages and cupboards and cellars; while outside is a lawn with rosery, filbert walk, two greenhouses (one with a vine), loose-boxes for ponies, lofts and a workshop, and garage for two cars! And for less than the present-day inflated price of a small pre-war four-square bungalow.

How did it happen? One summer day I was weary and dejected. By the roadside, where I sat listlessly, with a flat tyre on my car coming from London, I picked up a scrap of paper, saw an advertisement, on impulse walked to a telephone kiosk, rang up the agents, and found I was within a few yards of the house for sale.

So I knocked, entered (it was exactly 4 p.m.) and bought it at 4.3 p.m. There was a feeling in the house that made me act beyond my reason: the spirit of a place that is more real than most people may think.

October 25, 1945

AUCTION ON THE FARM

I thought I would not be able to see the auction sale on my Norfolk farm. There the implements were, laid out on the meadow; first the heaps of old wood and wire netting, the scrap-iron, old barrels, and broken chaff and fertiliser bags; then the better things, proceeding along the row until the smaller implements were reached, then the better implements, the valuable stack-cloths, and finally the rubber-tyred carts and trailers, the tractor, and the tractor implements.

A farm auction is rather like an old music hall show; the best turns come on later, when the house is likely to be full.

On the morning of the sale I was awake at five o'clock, waiting for the B.B.C. weather report, although on the window panes rain was lashing. I got up and went to the meadow, which was in places almost a lagoon, and the splashing place of happy ducks.

Some of the "items" were almost under water. Who would come to the sale on such a day? Who would buy my coils of Manila, rot-proof (pre-war) rope, my green stack-cloths, sheep-netting, who *could* draw off the heavy implements?

Already the entrance by the gate was a foot deep in mud. Also a great heap of barley on the asphalt floor of the barn needed turning over, it was "sweating" and might heat.

Eighteen tons to be turned over, four hours to the auction, and one-fifth of the items still to be carted out, aligned and labelled with their numbers!

Half an hour before the sale a solitary car had turned up, with a trailer. It belonged to the "diddecoys," as the gipsies who buy and sell old iron and all sorts of junk are called.

There they were, three of them, looking just as they had looked when I had attended the sale of the old tenant nine years before, when I was the "new man." Not a grey hair in their heads during those years; the same dark clothes, stove-pipe trousers, felt hat with turned down brims. Would they buy things for a shilling, worth several pounds? For there was no reserve on the various items. They were to go to the highest, which might also be the lowest, bidder.

At the advertised time of the sale it was raining so hard that trees a hundred yards away were dissolved in slanting grey. Other cars were arriving, parking off the roadway.

Five minutes later the auctioneer arrived, remarking cheerfully that it had been wonderful weather a week ago, but now perhaps there was

71

a little water in the meadow? At least, I said, the river had not yet burst its banks.

How about reserve prices on the best of the items, such as the tractor and the rib-rolls, the charlock-spraying machine, and tumbrils? Cheerfully he said that he would buy them in for me, if prices were too low.

By now 50 or 60 cars had arrived. It stopped raining. The wind even dried the wet on some of the plankwood. We started.

I followed the crowd, conscious of an empty stomach; somehow it was one o'clock, but the auctioneer, one eye on the clouds scudding overhead, kept them going from lot to lot.

It was surprising how some things made prices in excess of their value, while others went for almost nothing. Thus a butter-churn, almost new, converted to a seed-corn dresser (mercuric powder, against "smut") sold for 2s. only, while an ancient concrete mixer, which I thought might fetch £10 with luck, made over £60.

Then the horses were sold (poor old Smiler, Gipsy, and Gilbert) and the cows, with bullocks and calves, and at last it was over.

One thing gladdened me; so many small farmers came to me for advice about my own implements, asking if they were "all right;" a man is at his best when trusted by other men.

October 30, 1945

MOVING FROM A NORFOLK FARM

Here I am, in an old room with latticed windows, sitting at one end of a double-desk, on a high stool, and writing amid a jumble of tea-chests filled with unpacked books, office records, auctioneer's catalogues, empty bookshelves, Bible boxes, fishing rods, and big patch of damp in the ceiling. A slate blew off in the gale, and the rain came in.

The smaller boys are home for the half-term; and very useful they are. The bee-hives still stand, murmurous with air-fanning wings behind the perforated zinc shuttering, in the trailer, with the rest of the midnight load. In the "yard" stand carpenters' benches, rows of paint-pots, planks, a 20-ton heap of sawn logs, empty barrels, pails, corn-bins, and other stuff brought down to this Suffolk village from the Norfolk farm.

What a job it is, moving to-day. I have run over 1000 miles during the past ten days, through starlit nights, and over roads shrouded with fog, in rain and noon sunshine, slowly running south with loads and returning fast empty again.

Now most of the "clobber" is here, standing about the otherwise empty rooms, while outside the ducks and the hens scratch and squat within the wire-netting of the weedy garden. It's no joke moving from a farm!

We had to leave the baby behind, in the care of one who has helped us during the depressed years of the war. Little Sarah, with her one tooth, is coming south when we are in some sort of order.

Much of the furniture has been stored in the barn and granary of the farm since the migration from Devon eight years ago; we greet it now as an old friend, altered through the years, but still the same under the dust, the owl marks, the inquisitive nibble of mice teeth on the linseed-beeswax polish of long ago.

There is the Elizabethan linen press, with its hand-cut screw of ash, set in the dark oaken frame. Inside the little drawer Rikky found some fireworks, a Catherine wheel, a rocket, several flash-bangs, coloured flares, all pre-war and left over from a forgotten Devon high-go-glee party when we lived beside the salmon river in that West Country valley. They have been drying off in the cupboard beside the open hearth.

Down the two staircases, the voices of the small boys sound excitedly. They have just finished washing up, and are getting on their overalls to start unpacking the trailer. Their boots clop on the uncarpeted floors, and sound loud up here in my garret.

What else is there to say? I've got to rush away into the market town in a few minutes, to buy a flue-brush and also some fire-cement to mend the broken hot-water stove, the alternative is soot clinging to the thin cobwebs on the new-distempered walls and ceilings.

The hams want hanging, too; shrouded in their linen bags, they lie in a big wicker basket in the scullery, amidst pots and pans and boxes of crockery. The Silver Eagle has blown a gasket, and sparks fly past the three carburettors in the midnight runs; that, too, must be fixed, for the final journey tomorrow.

And what is that noise? Is it the village band practising? Strange honkings and clankings come down the chimney and through the open lattice window: quick, look out, it is a skein of wild geese passing overhead, flapping slowly, in a V-formation; are they white-fronts or brents?

I'll have time now to observe birds again, and also the ways of my fellow men; the farmer will have time to look at the landscape, to "stand and stare," in the words of the poet W. H. Davies, and not feel everlastingly the machine of business running through his head.

And now I must rush down the unfamiliar stairs and slip this in the postbox, and so to London and to you.

November 7, 1945

NOT SUCH A COMMON CAT

A small common-looking cat walked into the kitchen of the farm and settled itself on the coconut mat by the door.

It was a thin cat, little more than a kitten; a proper mongrel cat, with thin body, upstanding ears, yellow eyes, and its fur-pattern was a mixture of tabby, stripy and rabbit.

As the days went on, and it became obvious that the cat-kitten had adopted us, I invented for the smaller children a legend of how on our Home Hills, which abounded with rabbits, there lived a fearsome old buck whose aim in life was to hurt and kill poaching cats.

This fantastic buck-rabbit had learned to kill even stoats by a terrific kick of its combined legs; it had also learned to propel itself downhill on a roller-skate, which it shoved at a prodigious pace with its long, and muscular hind-legs. Hence the rabbit-like fur on the back of the new cat: it was an impression of fear, a sort of protective camouflage imprinted there when the cat was fleeing from the monstrous buck.

They did not believe it, of course, and greeted this bit of unnatural history with scorn; but the legend remained. The cat was called Eric.

Lean and ugly it might be, but Eric became a great ratter. In due course she produced some kittens and such was her personality that her name was not changed to the female Erica.

Eric was as good as any tomcat. She chased them out of the parlour when they came in with spits and savage curving claw-strokes. A dismal lot were the village toms; ears torn, paws maimed from being in rabbit-gins, and all with the hard yellow rat-catching eyes.

When a cat took to living rough in the woods, in rabbit-holes and hollow trees, its life was not of long duration.

One day another cat wandered into the farmhouse. She was gentle and pliable; unlike Eric, whom at times it was almost dangerous to stroke. The newcomer was a tortoise-shell, and a perfect armchair cat. In due course she produced a litter of kittens in the wastepaper basket, and these were transferred alongside Eric's, in a bushel-skep, or willow bullock-feeding basket, in an outhouse.

It was the time when long convoys of trucks and tanks were travelling, by night and by day, south along the coastal road. No questions asked, but we all knew it was for the invasion of Europe.

The coastal road by our farmhouse was very narrow; an inch or so over 13 feet; and the road curved dangerously there. Sometimes

75

lorries with five or six tons of gravel thundering north met a convoy of six-wheel lorries travelling south; then one heard the squeal of brakes.

Outside two columns were locked; motor bikes speeded; wheels moved slowly in reverse; and after an interval the convoys proceeded slowly again. After one such encounter the young tortoiseshell cat lay on the road, twitching. Eric saw her, and fled.

Robert was disconsolate for days. He appeared at meals with red eyes and pale face. Torty was his favourite. Rikky, more practical, buried her in the garden, and set up a small cross of willow (and, later in the year, some runner beans, hoping for a record crop).

Eric seemed to know what had happened. Ten minutes after the accident she was found in Torty's skep, feeding her kittens. Later she fed her own four. For some weeks she brought up the eight.

At last, we said, it would only be fair to the lean Eric to put the orphaned kittens down on the farm, and feed them on cow's milk, hoping that they would learn to catch the numerous mice in the corn-barn. We carried them down.

The strange thing was that Eric seemed to know they were there. We found her purring, lying on some sacks, while they drew nourishment from her. And twice every day she walked down the path through the gardens to the corn barn three hundred yards away, once every morning and again in the afternoon, and fed Torty's kittens. As regularly she returned and fed her own.

A very scarecrow of a cat, with lean flanks and her eyes grew harder than before, with their prolonged and intent staring for mice in the long grasses and rats slinking along the fences.

She did her job; all the kittens grew up well and strong. Ugly, "tisky," liable to bite if stroked too carelessly, Eric was a very common cat. She would have been laughed at in any Cats' Show. Since then she has brought up, a perfect mother, several litters.

November 14, 1945

THE LAKE OF SILVER LAUGHTER

What time it was I did not know, nor did I care. For the moment I had found peace.

Now peace is relative, being within, or not within, a man's spirit. One of the most peaceful days of my life was spent in a wood in late November, sitting at the base of a great oak tree and frying bacon, while bullets cracked through the branches above and sometimes a small shell shrieked and exploded in black smoke over the tracks trodden by many soldiers in the wood.

The German lines were about 100 yards away, in a field of frozen turnips beyond the edge of the trees. I was happy as I sat by my small fire, my tea made in the canteen, and the bacon frying.

Several soldiers, bearded and wearing balaclava helmets, were cooking their breakfasts under other trees. It was a scene of peacefulness, after the long and exhausting retreat from Mons, followed by the terrible fighting around Ypres.

At night the shadows of trees in the wood slanted with the rising white-green flares; wild duck flighted to the glistening pools of the shell-craters in the open marshy spaces; tiny charcoal braziers made of empty Maconochie ration tins, and swung on wire, revolved around the shadowy figures of soldiers at the redoubts and sentry posts.

I thought of that time this November night, as I walked among trees and heard the soft quacking and croaking of wildfowl on a lake which glimmered with distant lights around the perimeter of the park.

On the road lit with soft brilliance by those chains of lights motor traffic was moving, far enough away to emphasise the peace of the trees whose filigree branches arose dark against the luminous sky. The night air was still; a plane tree leaf slipping and twirling through the air was audible as it struck the path near me.

It was a mild night; there was no hint of frost; the smoke of burning heaps of leaves hung in the brumal air. You could have smelt a fox had he passed over the damp grass to the mice-runs, for his slightly rank hop smell would have lain thickly in the lower, damper layers of the mingled airs of that night.

Passing through the tallest trees which arose out of the grass of the park, I came to the edge of the lake itself, and saw the inverted image of the nocturnal scene shaking and shimmering across the water. Passing through the broad sheens of light were the dark shapes of teal and mallard, the pintails and the coots which were feeding and playing there. While all around me, but distantly, moved the lights of traffic, and above shone the faint stars of the metropolitan night, where on earth was there a scene of greater rest and peace?

And suddenly a wild cry of silver laughter rang out from over the waters of the lake. I had heard that lovely silver-bubble cry before, in other years, far away in the lakes of Canada.

It was the unmistakable cry of a loon, or Great Northern Diver. Those Canadian lakes at the fall: crimson maple leaves, immense silence of the grey rocky land whence the forest fires had passed and the season of ice was imminent; the last vermilion-bellied brook-trout taken on a Parmachene Belle in the deep water below the old logging dam; the ancient silence of the Indian-haunted air broken suddenly by the silver laughter of the loon . . . all this came back to me the other evening as I stood a moment in the peaceful quiet at the heart of London, in St. James's Park.

November 20, 1945

MUSIC OF THE PLOUGH

The boy who opens his first furrow behind a tractor does so with an immense zest and feeling of satisfaction.

The coarse noise of the engine is music in his ears – the music of his own power as he lifts the plough-breasts at the headland, steers along that margin of land to the next furrow of entry, and proceeds to cross the field again.

A feeling of benevolence comes to him as he watches the seagulls flying down to the feast he is giving them. These birds – usually black-headed gulls in winter plumage, that is, pearly-grey of head and wing and back (for the black feathers come on the poll at winter's end) – fly behind the up-screwing furrows in a series of spirals.

If he is observant he will note how this approach to the new-turned earth is made. Each gull as it alights, with red mouth open to scream its excitement, runs along the furrow, jostling with others to pull at worm or grub; the fortunate bird swallows rapidly, rises, flies to left or right of the line of the ploughing, gathers speed, and turns to sweep down again, perhaps to hang a moment, fluttering, a few inches from the breaking earth.

Sometimes the ploughman will notice a sudden silence in the raucous crying, and look round to see that the air is empty of white wings behind him. What has happened?

Perhaps as he goes forward, seeing the lines of furrows in further perspective, his eye will be caught by a white mark in the distance. Closing the throttle, and putting the tractor out of gear, and walking back, he may see a gull pinned down by the weight of earth. It may be by one wing, or the bird's head may be buried. In the jostle for food, it was a little too eager to seize a pink lob-worm.

Many a gull caught like this has been dug out of a furrow, held in the hands while it recovered, to fly slowly away.

Wild birds have no fear of a tractor crossing a field. I have sat on the iron seat of my machine and watched wood-pigeons from Scandinavia, the shyest of birds, walking a few feet away, with cock-pheasants, rooks, jackdaws and small migrants such as wagtails.

I have passed a hare, crouching in its form or scratched hole in an arable field, while cultivating in the early spring for a barley seed bed, so near that I could have touched it with a stick. Not the smooth form of hare or rabbit seen in pictures or behind the wire netting of a garden hutch, but an uneven angularity or tensity of wire-like sinews, a crouching polygon of fear; long black-tipped ears pressed back; large pale yellow eyes, set with staring black pupils, fixed ready to release into the blood-stream a glandular fluid or "boost" that would enable it to spring away with an abrupt and terrific acceleration.

It is not all fun and interest driving a tractor. In cold weather it becomes monotonous; the field seems so big, the machine so slow; the mind complains of the inaction.

The red sun of dawn becomes the red sun of evening; there is no end to the acres one must go up and down, up and down. The clothes and the skin smell of paraffin; the feet are always cold. I have known two youths who had to give up tractoring because of tuberculosis; and a third who, after six years, came to dread the work.

On my farm I hoped to be able to divide the work: the driver of the morning to work with his body at another job in the afternoon. But without technical knowledge the relief-driver was likely to damage the tractor.

It caused jealousy, too: the spirit of co-operation was not there. It was like the gulls, each for the biggest worm, scrambling and clashing behind the tail-wheel of the plough. And no farm, or any human venture, is any good without a co-operative spirit.

December 4, 1945

QUEST

Bank House, Botesdale in 1991

I

When I was younger I had a fine scorn of the ideas of my elders, with their crystallised wisdom, usually expressed in warning platitudes and proverbs. As a young man I wanted to find my own wisdom, and to make my own language to express it. I wanted nothing less than a new world. That was when I was unmarried, and living alone in a Devon cottage, after five years of war.

Now it seems that the years since 1921 have dissolved like clouds in the sky; and after another war I find myself ready to accept the old proverbs as the essence of human wisdom. Am I changed greatly from that ambitious and confident youth who set out to find the freedom of a new world after that far-away war?

Well, I have a large family of children. I have written several books. I have travelled over Europe and America; I have sought to find a new formula for living in farming half a square mile of land after reclaiming it from a near-derelict state; I have built my own home; and have been, in the eyes of the world, what is called a success. (Please don't misunderstand this; it is the job that counts, not what comes from doing it.) Anyway, what is "success?"

I sit here in the garret room of an old posting house, in the deep countryside sixty miles away from the land which I once reclaimed and made a "success" of. I planned when I took that land to found a yeoman family which would live there for generation after generation; it lasted eight and a half years.

Now it is ended, and I sit here in this high room, seeing the village street below through the old lattice panes of the eastern casement window. I find much pleasure in sitting here, writing at the tall, double desk which once belonged to a corn-merchant whose clerks were writing with quill pens when Dickens was writing his first stories. The floors of my garret room are of thick oak slabs, sawn and shaped by hand perhaps two hundred years ago. Or are they chestnut? It is hard to tell the difference between the two woods.

An electric fire warms my body, while winter rains lash the western casement window across the wide room. A radio gives soft music, as I write with a steel nib faintly scratching on the paper. I found the pen and nib in this old desk, where it has lain unused for years. A large watch, weighing over a pound, probably used by a railway guard in the last century, ticks as it hangs on a nail in the cream-distempered wall.

My books stand on the shelves in rows.

An extraordinary feeling of elation comes over me as I look around the room, with its new paint and clean walls; doors and woodwork of peat-brown, walls of cream-yellow, almost primrose. The ceiling is unspotted by fly or roof-stain; a smooth white over my head.

I ask myself again and again, am I really here, and is this lovely house really mine? Can my "luck" have changed so completely from that of a month or two ago, when all that I had worked for seemed to be breaking up, after holding together during one of the most terrible periods in human history – a period that was, and in a way still is, accompanied by much mental anguish? Do I truly see all the causes of that period plain, with their effects? For every effect has a cause, in personal life, as in the events of the world.

If it be true to say that poets and artists are, by reason of their extra sensitivity and clarity of vision, the unacknowledged legislators of mankind, to use Shelley's words, then, surely what happens to such men and women is also what is happening to the human world. Or is it an illusion to think that what happens to oneself – the real *inner* self, the still small voice of self – is only what is happening in the great world beyond one's personal sight and hearing? A raindrop on a twig after a shower holds an image of the landscape around it, a microcosm reveals within its small scope the macrocosm at large.

Therefore, writers who have learned, in self discipline, and by knowing and discarding their own prejudices, to be true to themselves are but expressions of an age. If the age is at variance within itself, such men will be at variance within themselves. But they will also see truth beyond the prejudices of an age. A prejudice is cramped truth; a one-sided fixed aspect of truth; truth that has lost its crystalline, its raindrop, quality.

As I look back, I see that I would not have been here, free to write, and therefore to fulfil my mission in life (however feeble the results), if a tractor engine on my farm had not broken its camshaft one day in June 1945. Spare parts were hard to find, but I learned that an engineer in the West Country had such a part. I farmed in the other side of England, in East Anglia. We needed the tractor; soon the harvest would be on. But – two hundred miles away! How to get the engine there quickly? Goods trains took weeks, maybe months. Well, it must remain broken, that was all.

At that time I was feeling the war-strain rather badly. What middle-aged person was not? My strain took the form of being unable to face up to any extra work, after eight years of striving to bring back the old British standard of craftsmanship which had been almost lost between the two wars.

And during the last year I had, during an enforced rest after coming out of hospital, worked as hard at my writing as I had previously worked on the farm. In twelve months I had written seven books with the inevitable result that, though the farm had been worked up to an "A" category I realised that I had paid the price. I *couldn't* do any more. Then the tractor broke.

It was no good giving way. Fortunately a friend came to stay, and with the help of my son, we got the engine into the small box-body of the old Silver Eagle, sports car which had been converted into an "agricultural lorry."

The next day I set off to the West Country. It was a fine day and the car ran well; we did the two hundred miles easily; arrived exactly on time at the works and delivered the engine. I was promised its readiness in a week's time, and after a meal left again for a further one hundred and thirty miles to a place I knew on the Atlantic Coast – and so to the woodland hut I had built years before on a hilltop. Now for a week's holiday, bathing, walks round the headland, the long stroll up the hill at night, seeing the lights of Appledore and Westward Ho again!

We all have our blind spots; we all tend to feel that the troubles of other people are not so real as our own. One morning I received a letter from my wife, saying she could not go on any longer in the old way. She said that although we had discussed the necessity of giving up the farm on scores of occasions, always they had ended in my saying that I would never give in; but things were getting worse every week, and she was going away, taking with her the baby and the younger children to an atmosphere where there would be less strain.

It was a shock to get that letter. My dream of founding a yeoman family, to last for centuries, was over – in eight short years. I tried to think objectively, but found it hard.

I knew my wife's bravery and capacity for self-sacrifice, and her habit of understatement, even of reticence, and I knew that for her to write like that, she had broken down. Eight years, 6 a.m. to 11 p.m., cooking, mending, looking after six children and a husband; dairy work and poultry; Women's Institute and playing the organ in church;

and hardest of all, perhaps, bearing with an artist who was fighting the
whole idea of war, striving for clarity in a darkening world. Yes, I
understood it. She ended that she would write later; meanwhile she
had left the farm.

For a year someone had been wanting to buy the farm, which I had
rebuilt and put in order. Should I sell it to him? I did not know what
to do, except to get home as soon as possible. I left my hut, with its
wide views over Exmoor, and turned the Silver Eagle eastwards again.

Having collected the tractor engine, I set out to cross England.
Half-way home the engine began to boil. It would not start again for
two hours. When at last I restarted it the engine was missing on
several of its six cylinders. Night came, and I had to stop by the
roadside without food. At dawn I restarted it, and it ran spluttering,
from town to village, down into valleys and painfully up hills. Sixty
miles from home the engine failed altogether.

II

I never believed in luck. I thought that "luck" was merely what a man
deserved by his own doings or efforts. Years of meditation had
revealed the qualities and defects of my own nature to myself; and I
knew that I had got from life exactly what I had deserved. If things
went wrong, I could blame only myself. And things had been going
wrong in my life for some time. My tenacity, my powers of endurance,
were waning.

Here I was, stuck by the roadside of an unknown village, beside a
car that had broken down. A grand car – once – but it was fifteen
years old. Heavens, the money I had spent, or misspent, on the Silver
Eagle! I could have bought a new car with it. And yet – it was an old
friend; its engine was sound, and people told me that it would yet
outlast a modern car of the cheaper sort, stamped out in the factory,
and falling to bits while the Silver Eagle was yet running.

But the trouble was, it wasn't running! An old friend? Take the "r"
out of "friend" and that was just what it was, I thought, my palm red
and blistered by swinging the handle in vain.

I sat on a cottage wall and drew a deep breath. This, I said to
myself, is the end. My farm is going downhill, my wife and family
have left, and now the Eagle is dud. I'm beaten.

But that was the very moment that my luck was to turn, though I did not know it at the time.

I began by saying that I never believed in "luck," but now, as I write about that day six months ago, from the cosy writing-room at the top of the new house, I am not so sure that a man's destiny is wholly in his own hands, for, as I lolled there, knowing that this was the trough of my depression, I noticed a bit of paper on the ground by my feet. It was a page of a local paper, as I saw when, idly, I picked it up for use as a cover to light my pipe with. I hadn't any matches, and remembered how an old Flemish peasant in 1914 had shown me, as a young soldier, how to light a pipe from someone else's cigarette by covering the top with the paper, clasping it to make it airtight, then making a small hole in the middle of the paper "drum," touching the hole with the cigarette end, and puffing, while the forced draught spread a crimson glow in the tobacco.

Before putting it on my pipe, I glanced at the printed column, which was headed: *Houses and Cottages for Sale.*

Without interest I read of one in a Suffolk village for sale with vacant possession. Seven bedrooms, two with powder closets; three living rooms; electric light and company's water laid on; kitchen with pitch-pine cupboards, oak floors and latticed windows; stabling for two ponies; garage for two cars; workshop and loft; garden of half an acre, with fruit trees, summer house, two green-houses, one with vine, lawn and rose garden. The whole in good repair and the house recently redecorated throughout. And for under £2,000.

Well, I thought, I know that "olde worlde" type of house, which is enchanting to read about, but awful to live in. Anyway, it must be sold fifty times over at that price, in June 1945!

Apply to the agents, in a town I had just come through in the Silver Eagle, its engine boiling and its quaint farm-lorry appearance – together with that of the old-fashioned driver – the cause of spontaneous merriment among all small children. Telephone number so-and-so.

Had I two pennies? If not, I would not bother. I was too weary to enter a shop and ask for change. I had two pennies in my pocket. Should I take a chance? There was a faded, red telephone box down the road. I walked slowly down to it. Like myself, the box appeared to have "had it." Its glass was splintered, the hinges of the door were rusty and squeaked as I pushed it open with my shoulder. Inside, I saw bullet-holes in the framework. Some after-pub exhilaration of browned-off troops? A passing man was smoking a cigarette, and I asked for the loan of the lighted tip. He told me that Jerry had sprayed the village street, mistaking it for the runway of one of the many air-stations round about, on the last raid on England of the war.

Two pennies and a sixpence got me to the agent's office. Was the house advertised for sale already sold? Not yet. Where was it? The voice of a girl, whom I thought to be intelligent (lucky Item No. 2), told me where it was. The name of the village meant nothing to me. I said I didn't even know where I was. The alert voice proceeded to a quick cross-examination.

Where had I come from? I told her. How far from that town? I said what I thought, in miles. Then, she declared, I was not far from the house. I said that the call-box was like a pepper-box, from the raid last March. Then you must be in the village where the house is, the voice said, and advised me to go up the hill and it would be on the left, a square, white house, one room of which was used for two hours weekly as a bank. I would find the worn brass plate outside.

Marvelling that things seemed to be going smoothly, I walked up the hill, my pulse quickening as I saw the house, just as the voice had described it. I did not hesitate. I knocked.

Almost at once the door opened, and I was invited into a lounge with black beams and what looked to be a bow-fronted window. It was cool, with a new cream distemper on a new, rough-surfaced wall-paper. A quick glance and we were through into a hall lit by a skylight, and thence into a passage with a glass garden door, and a view of a smooth lawn, roses in bloom, and a new-painted green-house beyond. Another room, with an oak beam crossing the ceiling, an open brick hearth, deep cupboards each side of the hearth, and a glass door leading elsewhere.

"Would you care to see the rest of the house now, or have some tea first?"

A sense of urgency was on me. I said I would like to see the house. Into another room, with a view of the garden, the breakfast-room; then up the stairs, lit by two windows and to three light bedrooms; sound floors; all exquisitely decorated. Up a smaller stairway, to a window overlooking fields and trees and red-tiled roofs, and so to three oak-floored bedrooms.

One was large, with lattice windows, decorated in heather-brown moorland brown with primrose walls. The windows looked east and west, for the rising and the setting of the sun. The very place for my books, my double corn-merchant's desk! A third stairway, leading down to a smaller room below, oak and lattice windows, a secret bedroom for the author to creep to after writing what zestful books in the room above! After nearly nine years of slaving night and day on a farm, what peace, what relaxation!

Big cupboards, with hand-cut pegs inside; down another stairway and suddenly into the kitchen, with modern range, two pitch-pine cupboards, and iron tie-rods crossing the ceiling, excellent for drying baby clothes upon. Down a cool passage to the large scullery, where was a hot-water boiler, a copper, sink with four taps – rainwater, drinking, hot and cold – and through another door to the bathroom, painted in white, with an open corner cupboard and four shelves.

Yet another door, opening to a courtyard with filbert hedge, a baytree, and the small stables. So through a fifth door to the garden, one green-house hung with grapes, and another where grew luxuriant tomatoes. Down a garden path set with clipped box-hedge border, and so to a wistaria tree in bloom, and a garden door leading to a quiet lane below steps.

I had been in the house and garden about three minutes. I thought furiously, and, a few moments later, I said suddenly: "I will buy it."

"It's a good roof," said my host. "Oak rafters, all sound. I don't think you will regret buying it. Several people are after it . . . or were. Well, I've bought and sold several houses in my time but never one so quickly as this."

My mind was now eager to find my wife, to tell her that our troubles were over. But where was she? I had not the slightest idea. I went out into the street again, and with renewed hope, swung the starting handle. The engine started at once, and I set out for the Norfolk farm, intending to sell it that very day to someone who had wanted to buy it for over a year.

III

I had found a house where we might all live when the farm was sold; now I had to find the family. The only address I knew was c/o a firm of solicitors in the south of England; and I did not want to write to them, as I knew that certain people were interested in keeping us apart until a divorce petition was filed and a decree perhaps made absolute. I saw it all in perspective; war-strain; there would be thousands of similar cases now the war was ended, and the reaction to war-strain was unsettling many who had held on during the six woeful years.

As I sped home to the farm, in the Silver Eagle, I wondered if the B.B.C. would be putting over realistic talks to men soon to be demobilised, and to their wives, telling them frankly that they were bound to feel an estranging difference, even a chill of hopelessness, at the start of trying to settle again in "civvy street." Every action has its reaction; every time a gun is fired it recoils with an equal and opposite force, though that force is diffused. Likewise, any sustained action brings an equal and opposite feeling of reaction, to cause disappointing emotions, liable to be misinterpreted by inexperienced people.

I knew that my domestic "tragedy" was part of the reaction from the long strain of the past seven years; and I knew it was right for me to give up the farm and work only at my writing, and to bring the family together again. I would not admit defeat; and as I felt the blame was almost entirely mine, the cure lay almost entirely in my hands. And having found out that my wife and family were in the north of England, thither I set out one Saturday morning.

Before I left the farm in Norfolk, I fitted to the Silver Eagle another magneto that I had bought at a car-breaker's dump. The effect on the engine literally was electric: it was a greyhound where before it had been a crippled tortoise. The day was fine, my heart lightened as I sped along the flat and curving roads of Lincolnshire, seeing fine crops of corn and sugar-beet, where in pre-war years there had been acres of red, blue, and yellow flowers (the bulb farms of Little Holland), and so to the rising ground before Grantham and the Great North Road.

I stopped at The Angel in Grantham to have a pint of beer in the room where, as a young soldier nearly thirty years before, I had made merry with my friends before going out to the battle of the Somme. I confess I felt more nervous now than I did in those far-away years: and after a silent toast to the shadowy faces, I went outside, started the engine, and the low, rakish, black, open car moved swiftly up the broad road leading to Yorkshire.

That night I stayed with friends in Wakefield; and the next day, being Sunday, I telephoned to the châtelaine (with whom I was acquainted) of the house outside Selby, and making my voice as steady and pleasant as possible, announced who I was, adding that I was staying a few miles away, and did she think that I might come over that afternoon and see the children? Perhaps she would tell me if Loetitia (my wife) would rather I did not come?

"Yes, do come, and bring your friends to tea," replied the voice. "Here is Loetitia; she will speak to you."

I thought how an alert, cheerful quality had come into Loetitia's voice since last I had heard her speak six weeks before. She sounded happy.

"The baby is so well, and putting on weight at last," the voice said. "And Rikky has learned to ride. He was saying only yesterday: 'If only Dad could see me gallop Bunty round the paddock. . . .' It is so lovely here for the children. Right, we will expect you sometime in the afternoon; we have tea at four-thirty."

Now my two Wakefield friends had been with me in Devon, where they had been spending their holiday, during the first two weeks of June. I had made their acquaintance on the sands, and from the first we had been inseparable. We had bathed and walked together, played skittles in the pub at night, and gone in their S.S. car to visit Lynton and Lynmouth.

We had made a perfect holiday trinity. We had laughed and joked, free of business and family worries for the time being. We had come home on moonlit nights across Exmoor, listening to symphony concerts and dance music from behind the dashboard coming with a startling clarity – music as though heard for the first time – while the lights in lonely moorland cottage windows glowed along the lanes as we glided by, feeling free after the long years of blackout. But all holidays end; and my friends had gone back to the industrial North, with promises that we would meet again sometimes and continue our trinity of friendship.

I mentioned this as it is significant; had they not happened to live a few miles from where Loetitia had gone in her unhappy weariness, to find rest and peace after the trying years, I do not think I could have summoned up enough hope, or will-power, or inspiration, to integrate myself sufficiently to make the journey to Yorkshire at that critical time.

For the family *malaise* was but part of the general decline in hope which had been slowly reducing my vital powers ever since the end of the 1914-18 war, when as a demobilised soldier I had hoped that a new world of human understanding and regeneration would come to being. All my books, even those dealing with "Nature," had had that one theme, and I had lived to see, and to feel within myself, that all that I, and my friends of the "lost generation" had aspired to in our various ways, come to nought; some of us in the recent war to be looked at askance, and even suspect in perfidy to the England we loved, and once shed our blood for.

Had it not been for a chance acquaintanceship on the Devon seashore in June of that year, I would not have gone to Yorkshire in the following August; and thereby I might not even now be alive to write these words.

Is there a pattern behind the seeming chaos of life? As an artist in the twenties I aspired to this faith in a pattern of the "eternal verities;" in the thirties I doubted myself; now in the forties I feel that faith is firm in me for the rest of my life on earth, whatever may happen to me personally.

On that Sunday afternoon we left Wakefield, a town of industrial smoke upon which one day the sun will shine clearly as it did centuries ago on those beautiful Yorkshire uplands, and went through Pontefract and along the grey roads to the wooden toll-bridge over the River Ouse at Selby. We passed a mill advertising "flour white as snow," while I wondered if one day it would be advertising "flour gold as the wheat-berry" – for, believe me, whole-wheat bread is the staff of my optimistic life, while white flour was the broken reed of my former pessimistic existence.

Soon we were turning off the road, and approaching a lodge and going down a war-rutted drive leading to a house with grey towers and overgrown tennis courts. The wheels of the car slowed on the grassy gravel, and there was young Rikky running across a paddock to the iron railings of the park, holding a jam jar in which swam minnows he had just netted from a pond. And there, under an old ash tree, lay Baby Sarah in her pram, waving a chubby brown leg with spread toes, while her open blue eyes were as serene as the sky. Then from the tiled porch of the house, Loetitia in a tweed coat and skirt was coming to greet her guests, with tall daughter Margaret, dark-eyed and with her mother's peach complexion, by her side. Feeling fine-drawn and a little quivery, I walked forward slowly to meet them.

IV

Just to explain briefly the sort of person I am – and why I have the reputation, among some people, of being, well. . . . As I see it, does anyone *really* know himself?

I suffered in early youth a shock which altered my entire conception of "seeing" human life.

It happened on Christmas Day, 1914, when a youthful volunteer of seventeen years of age in the British Expeditionary Force found himself staring tremulously at soldiers in muddy field-grey uniforms standing in what a few hours before had been the dreaded and mysterious No Man's Land.

Hitherto, this youthful self had not thought of the *Allemands* who sniped and fired machine-guns, or lay out in strange, motionless shapes among the turnips of a forsaken field, as human beings like himself; yet abruptly he was among their living reality on the hard, frozen Flemish field, where they were smilingly offering English soldiers gifts of cigars and cigarettes, and receiving in return bully beef and slabs of chocolate. It was miraculous! Some of the Germans spoke English, and exchanged addresses with our chaps for "after the war." "Good luck, English comrade!"

One young Saxon I spoke to declared that Germany could never lose the war, as they were "fighting for the right, for civilisation," a statement that puzzled me greatly, for *we* were "fighting for the right, for civilisation."

"*Ach* no, English comrade. You are mistaken!"

"But no – it is you who are mistaken!" We smiled at one another, not wishing the other to be embarrassed.

Out of that incident I began to think for myself.

The war ended; I left the army. I began to read many books of beautiful prose and poetry (including the New Testament), and so discovered to my joy that an idea which in my ignorance I had thought myself alone to have discovered, was no new idea at all; on the contrary, it was the theme of all great art and religions among all races of mankind.

Could it be that I, an imperfectly educated and obscure soldier of the war, was destined to be one of those artists and seers like Shelley, Keats, Shakespeare, Tolstoy, Thomas Hardy, Paul of Damascus, Joan of Arc, Beethoven, and Rembrandt? Was it my destiny to reveal that modern civilisation, with its fearful irruptions of civil strife and periodical wars, its slums, unemployment, and family dissensions needed an entirely new basis of thought, an entirely new economic system in order to free and develop the social instinct in human beings, to give them the fuller life dreamed by the visionaries of known history?

In the emotion arising from this thought I found life in London unbearable, so I left for the remote countryside in Devon, there to meditate and clarify my thoughts during long walks in the sunshine of the lanes and fields, to receive inspiration in the timeless surge of the sea, from the everlasting azure of the sky.

I lay on my back in the meadows and watched the piled majesty of white cumulus drifting remotely through the blue halls of the wind. I was out of doors most of the day and the night, absorbed in the vastness of sunsets, inspired by the water-dim clarity of dawn. How could the new way of life be brought into the minds of millions of people – the new world where all would be wide friendliness and trust, because every man would have faith in himself, out of a naturally developed instinct in man's higher destiny?

This new way could only come from early contact of children with Nature; the pure thoughts given by the elements must be the philosophical basis of the new world. Every child must have a fair chance, not be warped, as at present, by the economic system, and so often ruined in thought and body by inevitable frustration.

I go back a quarter of a century in writing this, to explain that if I had not "gone into the wilderness," I would never have cleared myself of ordinary prejudices; never learned to trust my inner mind despite derision and disapproval. I would never have developed the faculty of seeing human complication as simple in origin; never taught myself, by trial and error, to use words to convey my thoughts.

After some years of solitary living and writing in obscurity, I awoke one morning to see my name printed in all the newspapers on the same day, and in two London dailies my work was the subject of a "leading article." To be truthful I was not surprised, for I had known myself ever since finding, long assessed, the talent which by some accident of heredity had been born into my physical body. I had believed the dead poets and writers whom I felt to be yet living, whose spirits encouraged and affirmed me; but what I had not reckoned were the effects on my human personality of sudden material success.

As I moved among charming and amusing people, I began to see my previous ideas as others had seen them in the past: as arising from a "half-baked" individual whose ideas came merely from inexperience. (Shades of the first battle of Ypres!) I strove to become "normal," to rejoin the herd; but I failed to qualify on their standards. So I was neither one thing nor the other.

This phase was succeeded by one in which I saw the flux of life as a struggle wherein the mental clarity of the visionaries was inevitably frustrated by the stupidity and selfishness of the majority, unless the visionary used all of his arts and latent powers to overcome the mental darkness of the human world.

So inevitably the wanderer on the Devon hills became a political partisan. The vision of Christmas Day had become an active struggle against the dark forces which would bring about another world war. Those who did not agree were against the truth; those who did not think as I did were part of the dark, unknowing force that was helping to prepare the next war.

It was the strain of bearing this appalling thought through the decade before the war, and through the hellish frustrations of the war itself, that had made my family life finally unbearable to my wife; for she did not think as I did. Therefore, as I walked with her in that Yorkshire garden I could not plead for myself, for at least I had no illusions about my behaviour; the impersonal artist in me was determined to be on her side.

I told her about the house I had bought for her and the children, saying that when I had seen them all safely settled in – providing she wanted to live there, of course – I would go away. "You needn't decide now," I said. After a pause, she remarked: "The farm was too much for you with all that writing you did as well."

"I wrote seven books in the last ten months, because I felt the night was coming, and I must get them done while I could. But that doesn't excuse my behaviour."

"You see," she said, "I was afraid for the children."

"I was afraid, too."

Baby Sarah was now opening her blue eyes under the ash-tree. Her legs were brown, and not so woefully thin as when I had seen her last. "She is taking her bottle better now," said her mother. Rikky, wearing a Yorkshire coal-miner's hat – *ersatz* for bowler – was revealing how he could ride Bunty, the pony, round the paddock. Tall daughter

Margaret was walking, with one arm linked in her mother's and another in her father's, to see the stables and the horses.

Was I really there? Was it but a dream? I felt like a man let out of prison, as we strolled through lines of corn-stooks in the harvest field – then into the house for tea: a table surrounded by R.A.F. faces with wives and children.

Then good-bye, with smiles and a mutual hope of a new beginning, and the firm feeling that there was immortal harmony above the seeming chaos of human life; even as the spirit of that faraway Christmas had endured through all the mental anguish of the second war of a lifetime.

V

If you remember, I said that when I went to see the family in Yorkshire, I watched my small son, Rikky, riding a pony called Bunty round the paddock, while Rikky wore on his head, as substitute for the correct bowler or "pot hat," a helmet of the type used in coal mines. You've probably seen the kind of thing in pictures, close-fitting, rather like a small old-fashioned coal-scuttle – black, fibrous, tough, yet light, resembling a crash helmet. The idea was that Rikky, if pitched off the pony (after all he had been riding only six weeks), would save his scalp.

Now Rikky is perhaps an unusual small boy. He does not mind wearing eccentric clothes or hats. Thus at times he is to be seen under a red and green head covering, generally worn by coloured men picking cotton under the hot sun of Alabama or Georgia; a cap with a long peak, a cross between a jockey's cap and the sort of hat a grasshopper might wear, if grasshoppers ever became hat-conscious.

Rikky does not mind the criticisms of other small boys – indeed, they do not criticise him. His amiable temperament, added to a power of imagination, his lack of competitive spirit, usually make him the leader in any venture with other boys. In the Norfolk village the local boys were fairly nice children. It was an excellent village school; I rarely heard swearing, never saw any fighting, but there was a lot of smiling. Rikky was president of the Kestrel Club, which had a hide-out on the Home Hills, where usually a fire was made and potatoes and sausages cooked and eaten in the fingers.

Rikky sometimes wore, in the old days on the farm, a green deer-stalker hat, with flaps that could, in the cold shear of east winds, be tied over the ears. It was the kind of hat Sherlock Holmes was reputed to have worn. I bought it before the war for myself to wear when I should go shooting wildfowl on the marsh, but I seldom wore it, as the double peak at the back stuck into my shoulder-blades when I looked up at the sky, and the hat invariably tilted off. It was a deer-stalker hat, for crawling down mountain-sides and preventing the rain from trickling down the neck; no use on the flat marshes of Norfolk.

So I gave it to Rikky, thinking it would look picturesque and nicely old fashioned on the small, dark head of the seven-year-old. To my surprise his owl-eyes opened wide with pleasure, and: "Coo, *thanks, Dad!*" he exclaimed. And he wore it about the village, without comment.

It was the same when I presented to him that coal-miner's helmet on the Sunday afternoon in Yorkshire. Did he "eye it askance," did his cheeks turn red, his eyes downcast with apprehension that once more his dictatorial parent was forcing upon his shoulders a bizarre and eccentric headgear? Did he protest with white face and tight lips that it was hardly the thing to wear in the best horsy circles; a compressed paper oval dome with electric torch attachment for working a thousand feet beneath growing grass?

No, Rikky's brown eyes lit with joy. He smiled, and there was his usual enthusiastic, "Thanks, Dad!" And forthwith Rikky set it on his head, gave an excited cry of "super," and set Bunty in slow motion, while he held the reins correctly, hands low, his knees well in and heels turned out, just as Miss Charlton had schooled him in many quiet hours.

I had been given that black, pudding basin hat a short time before. A friend asked if I would like to go down a coal-mine, and I had accepted. After changing my clothes at the pit-head and putting on a suit of overalls I always carry when I drive the old Silver Eagle, we entered a massive, iron bucket hanging on a cable over a shaft, and were let down into circular brick-lined gloom. As we descended, I wondered if I would feel any pressure on my ear-drums, as when descending the lift of the Empire State or Rockefeller Buildings in New York. There the pressure increases so noticeably as the lift flicks down past the scores of floors that you must open your mouth, lest your ear-drums crackle with the increase of density. But this descent into a hole in the Yorkshire ground was so gentle that it might have been a couple of feet instead of four hundred.

That was a new shaft; they were preparing it for new machinery, but later we went down an old shaft. There the lifts descended at thirty m.p.h. until we had gone down over a thousand feet. Pressure was maintained behind wooden flap-doors; the ears on entering were buffeted. We walked half a mile beside a conveyer belt bringing back coal which had been picked and shovelled from the coal-face ahead, and as we hobbled along I noticed paper bags of some white powder lying at intervals beside the shored-up wall of the tunnel. This was powdered limestone, which was spread on the coal-dust we walked on as a measure against fire arising from friction of passing feet. We turned corners, we sweated, and came at last to the coal seam.

The seam here was only nineteen inches thick. That meant to get to the "cragging lip" we had to shove ourselves along on our sides, using elbows and boot-welts. It was extremely hot; my electric torch showed that the coal had lain pressed between grey rock, a thin layer in a sandwich. Every few feet, a wooden prop was wedged between top and bottom of the grey rock, to take the pressure. There were billions of tons pressure above us. We scraped along a nineteen-inch cavern while now and again a larch pit-prop, only about four inches thick, gave a sudden ominous crack.

Right up at the cragging lip men were lying on their sides, heads held back, using compressed-air drills to break the coal into lumps and flakes. Six hours of that work, in heat and dust, with pit-props liable at any moment to shatter and splinter – another headline in the newspapers. Having done a certain amount of hard work myself on occasions, I could appreciate what those chaps did, and why, when the shift came up in the rushing cages, lean men with faces pallid under the sweaty coal dust, did not speak as they trooped to their numbered lockers by the shower-baths. I noticed that the lockers were painted in various colours, so were the sections of the hundreds of shower-baths. Reason, to avoid congestion at the entrances; a green-locker man sought a green shower, and a blue, a blue. Whose splendid idea was that? Someone who knew what it felt like to be all-in, grimy, thin-eyed, ghostlike after the sweating out below.

Miners, I was told, did not have extra rations, but they could get good meals in the canteen. But after a shift, my friend said, a miner didn't want to hang about in the canteen; he wanted to get home. You

can't do that work underground on ordinary rations, any more than
your car can run without petrol. If you take out you've got to put back,
whether it be the soil, human nature, or what you will. "Something
for nothing" is no good; it leads straight to the atom bomb.

VI

I had always wanted to explore the dales of Yorkshire, ever since a
drive in the Silver Eagle on a bitter day of January years ago, when I
travelled north from London to Cumberland, to stay at an inn near
Coniston Water, and follow the foxhounds on foot across the moors
and under the fells. Those were the days of free motoring, and eggs
and bacon in the inns whenever you felt hungry.

My companion of that far away time and I got to the Sunne Inn at
twilight; it had been a long and cold drive, for the car was a sports
model, and we had the hood down. The idea of a hood was scorned in
those days; there was no need to be cold, despite the biting, clear
winds sometimes swirling with dry sleet, for we both wore leather
flying coats with fur collars, flying helmets, goggles, and horse-hide
gloves which I had brought back from the United States a year or two
before. Even so, the journey had been one to endure; we had far to go
before twilight, with a report of snow falling over the breadth of
Yorkshire.

So it was fast driving under the lovely grey-green fields of
Wensleydale, famous in old times for its little round cheeses. Under a
louring sky we sped at between fifty and sixty miles an hour,
sometimes touching seventy on straight and empty lengths of grey
road. It was exhausting work, but in the thirties one was always
hurrying, speed was the great thing; life had a hectic rhythm all over
the world. Man was hastening away from "reality" (which meant
himself), trying to escape his thoughts in movement; or swarming in
masses which found an outlet for energy in marching, speeches,
counter-marching and speaking. We know what came out of that
mental trend, when the "intellect" had debunked the illusions of the
body, when artificial stimulation and then more stimulation was the
idea, and what was sufficient in the past was not good enough for the
present . . . it all came to a clash in 1939.

So in 1945, when I found myself in Yorkshire, and my friends suggested a journey into the dales one Sunday, I pleaded that we should not travel too far, or too fast. Could we not walk?

Petrol rationing automatically limited distance; and we proceeded away from Wakefield in a northerly direction, intending to get away from the pall of sombre cloud which overhung the coal country, into the sunshine of the green uplands. We went to Wharfedale, following the river which swirled and slid over its rocky bottom until we left the car under a tree and proceeded on foot along a pathway beside the stream.

What a relief to leave a closed car behind, and walk on foot! That is a return to the natural life, away from an unnatural civilisation. The lungs open and close with the swing of arms and the movement of the legs; blood courses in arteries; veins bring it back to be purified by the oxygen extracted by the lungs. Stoop by the beckside and touch the water with your fingers, scoop it up in the palm, feel how its brightness is charged with oxygen; water that is *living*.

Did you see that trout leap after the waterfly dancing over the pool below that chasm in the rocks? Imagine that strong and happy fish, its golden-brown scales set with vermilion spots, in one of the dead streams of the towns, and within a few moments it will be twisting and gasping on its side, turning belly-up as its eyes film with asphyxiation. Where living water is dead through pollution, human life also is correspondingly frustrated.

Consider that sight yesterday in the teashop. Of two blue-eyed children sitting at a table, their waxen faces lined with sleeplessness, putting out little hands to take the fried potato chips from the plate. Mother slapping them petulantly, Father scowling; Mother making a sudden scolding remark to him, he turning away with an oath. Children, between three and five years old, jittery and all anyhow; already ruined as human beings – the matrix of their minds formed in emotional chaos – grinned at one moment, scolded the next, giggled at nervously a moment afterwards; a tight-lipped slap, a thin grizzling whine from lost children.

A by-product of a chaotic industrial world . . . leading to a sudden revelation four times as bright as the sun itself – the sun which is the giver of life, truth, and beauty? Who dares to think of that revelation, to see it steadily, and see it whole, in terms of his or her own defects? Or does all action based on the intolerable wrongness of such human spoliation lead only to Golgotha?

In ancient days living water was the symbol of rebirth, of the new consciousness, and baptism was a ritual or outward sign of the affirmation of the idea of a new world coming by way of self-regeneration.

Here is the sun shining on the pool, the rings of the trout spreading to the channered rocks – scooped and hollowed by the living water during hundreds of centuries, of winter rains running down the hills into the dale and surging down the rocky bed of the valley.

Do we work all our lives so that in the end we may escape from the sombre clouds and the polluted streams, finally to see the living water, to enjoy the clear sunshine and hear the songs of the birds in the beeches and rowans, as though for the first time? And in the struggle to escape, do we lose the faculty of clear enjoyment; or is it perhaps warped in us while we are yet between three and five years of age?

I am sorry if these thoughts obtrude on what perhaps should be an account of a happy day in a Yorkshire dale. But can a man live only for himself? There are two opposed theories in the world now, and some think they may one day come into conflict. One says that if man minds his own business, and looks after himself, without interference in the lives of others, he will be happy and leave a minimum of unhappiness about him; the other declares that man must not live for himself alone.

I wish I could be sure of the answer; but I do know that whenever I walk in personal freedom under a clear sky, when I stoop to feel the beauty of living water, I can never forget those who live under the sombre clouds.

VII

At last the day came for me to bring the family home from Yorkshire, from the old house where they had been staying so happily for three months. It was now September; our harvest on the Norfolk farm was over. The eldest boy, who had stayed with me and "seen the corn brought in," was nineteen; the farm was sold; we would be quitting at Michaelmas, for the new farmer to move in. My eldest son had worked as hard as any boy in England during the past six years. He had left school at thirteen years of age, when the war broke out. Now he was nineteen, and what was his future?

People had criticised me for taking him away from school in September 1939. In those days I had confidence that my action was right. I saw, in my mind, a great change coming over England, either from the war itself or from the after effects.

The great City of London, with its money-power built up during the years since the beginning of the Industrial Age, its vast international trade which once had ruled the world, could not keep that supreme place which had been consolidated since the overthrow of Napoleon, the first of the continental dictators to challenge the money-power of Lombard and Threadneedle Streets.

I saw the decline of the export trade from England; I saw a return to the land, to a less complicated way of living. Money would not mean what it had meant in the past; only by hard work would England be able to live. In other words, the system of education was based on the idiom of the City of London; everyone strove to get a job in an office or other place where hard bodily work need not be done. That was no good.

Life was like a vast mushroom; a thin stalk supporting a great swollen head. Before the war everyone was trying to get into the head, out of the stalk, without which there could be no life in the head. I saw that head falling off an attenuated stalk. I saw a future of hard, rigorous living for people in England; privilege gone; and the basis of all living on the earth was the land.

My boy could be a farmer. I had the land; I was putting it in order from a derelict state; the war was started. Let the sun and the living air over the fields teach him; let him forgo algebra and Latin and learn instead how to build a corn-stack, plough a straight furrow, grow a sugar-beet, and prune an apple tree. That was the dream.

What went wrong, during those six years of the war? I think, as I knew at the time (but could not do anything about it, being in the thick of things that never stopped or "let up"), that he had too much put on him too early. There were seventy acres of swampy meadow and old grass to drain; miles of twenty-year overgrown hedges to cut and lay; roads to be built; one hundred and thirty acres of weedy arable to make clean and bring back into fertility. The farmhouse had to be made out of some dark, damp cottages. I hadn't enough money to do this – apart from the physical labour – unless I wrote at night.

All work and no play. . . . My son and I often worked all through Saturday afternoons and Sundays, while I strove constantly to form his mind away from the careless idiom of the village which, ever since the last war, had been "let go," many of its men out of work, and dispirited. Then the bomber air-stations started to be built, and labour was scarce. Boys leaving school at fourteen could earn six and seven pounds a week there.

But my boy was a good boy; he stuck to the job of ploughing seven days a week, without pay – for the bank account was overdrawn and to keep down the overdraft we regarded the farm as a family unit – and looked forward to the time when, with his other pals in the village, he would be joining the R.A.F. He was an A.T.C. cadet. Many a time he finished work on the farm a few minutes before Sunday dinner, hurried home, washed and changed, swallowed some food, and dashed off on his bicycle to a parade, while I went back to the tractor.

I am told that we did in six years what was half a lifetime's work: twenty years' work. But one has to pay for such overwork. I thought as I drove the eight h.p. Ford saloon to the Yorkshire house that a greater crisis had probably been averted when my wife had left on that June day. For it had forced me to give up the task of trying to make a hilly, awkward farm – which had broken many a farmer in the past – into something which, by its very nature, it could never be.

Now I looked forward to a new life in the house I had bought in Suffolk. There I could have my books, my desk, and my prints on the walls; most of them had been lying unpacked in damp tea-chests during the eight years of our pioneering. And my wife could rest, and perhaps take a country walk that did not have an urgent purpose behind it.

There she sat, in the front seat of the Ford, Baby Sarah in her arms, a light blue, woollen cap on the little fair head with its wisp of hair behind, tied by a minute blue ribbon. Sarah was six months old, and her pigtail was only an eighth of an inch thick and an inch long, but the ribbon was a gesture! Margaret, fifteen years old, was going back to school from Yorkshire; so the three younger boys sat in the back seats.

We got home in the late afternoon, and that evening we sat at the long refectory table, while the face of Mrs. Valiant, our faithful friend and wife of Tom the teamsman, beamed as she came in with the roast chicken. Dear Mrs. Valiant, if all in Britain had her spirit, we would never have got into the muddle we have all lived through.

All lived through? No, we do not forget those who will never return;

among them Mrs. Valiant's son who, with the Norfolk regiment, died in Thailand. Bless you, dear Mrs. Valiant, you saw us through our troubles, which were small compared with your own secret anguish during those dark years; and when we saw a gleam of light at last, you had to bear the hardest blow that a mother has to bear; and you bore it with a smile behind the tears; for, despite all, you had faith.

VIII

To move from a farm where you have spent many years of your life in hard work, overcoming difficulties but to face new ones, where your children have grown up and you have dreamed of your son following on when you retire, is to face, at moments, an almost overwhelming sense of poignancy and regret. There is no need to dramatise the situation to yourself; its chill and vacant realities are possessing you, though outwardly this may not be apparent. I do know that when finally I had undertaken to sell my farm I turned away from the telephone and wept as though I had heard that England had been defeated in the war.

So all had been in vain. The thousands of hours in the wind and rain and sun, building cottages, making roads, digging flints from a pit with blistered hands, sweating in the hot sun clad only in shorts and socks and shoes, making new roadways up hills and carting by horse and lorry thousands of tons of gravel; pulling thousands of tons of black mud and reeds from choked and overgrown dykes; cutting acres of congested thistles and docks; felling miles of twenty-year over-grown thorn hedges; striving with board-dams set aslant in the trout stream to clear the polluting sludge poured in from drains and culverts, to make the river sweet and clear as it had been in the days before the world turned sour with the effects of high finance; quarrying fifteen hundred tons of chalk and spreading them patiently on the arable, to bring back the needed lime to grow corn and sugar-beet; the plans for planting trees in groups, and restoring the woods which had never recovered from the fellings of the 1914–18 war; the plans for a new farmhouse with a great hall for dancing and harvest supper on the Home Hills; for making a yeoman's paradise out of one of the beautiful valleys of the coastal country of East Anglia, where my grandchildren would meet once every year in family union and we would drink home-made wines and eat our own wheaten cakes and butter and hams. All had been in vain.

Then I thought of how the land lasts, though individuals perish; and I thought of other men, many of them so much younger than myself, who were lying in the sands of North Africa and the jungles of the Orient, or floating in the seven seas. In vain?

While I sat alone in the little studio where my books were ranged in rows on the shelves and the hams in muslin bags hung from the beams overhead – we had made this studio from a derelict small barn in the garden of my cottage – Loetitia came to me with a tray of tea. After a while, as we sat there drinking tea, I asked her if she felt sad at leaving the farm. She gave me a steady, reflective look, and after an interval said quietly that she was looking forward to the new house. I had seen that look in her eyes when we left our Devon home nearly a decade before, and the thatched house in the valley where our children had been born. Then she said quietly:

"I am in your hands." A moment later: "I am glad for your sake that now you will be able to rest and think only about your writing. Don't you worry, dear; things will be all right. Won't it be lovely to be able to sit before the fire, or work in the garden, and to know there is no outside worry?"

The auction sale of the farm implements had been fixed, and the vans for the removal of the furniture ordered. Then followed a hectic period which was in a way a recapitulation of all that had gone before. The lorry had to be painted, the battered wings hammered out and sprayed; the tractors to be advertised, cleaned, put in order; hundreds of spare parts sorted out and listed; carts, trailers, ploughs, rollers, harrows, elevators, barrels, rolls of wire netting, seed-drills, cultivators, ladders, corn sacks; in all, hundreds of items set to rights. There were thirty tons of branches of oak, thorn, ash, guelder, and elm to be sawn into logs by the circular saw, piled, and transport arranged for the sixty-mile journey into Suffolk. All the books to be packed into those tea-chests of three-ply wood in which they had travelled from Devon; and furniture to be got ready.

And the problem of "junk" to be resolved. What was junk and what was necessary in the new home? One item was several thousand square feet of yew-wood planks which had come from Devon, one day to be made into tables, cupboards and bookcases. It was stored in the corn barn, and had been cut from trees many centuries old on the hills above the Devon valley. Some said the yews had been planted there by the knight who had carried William of Normandy's shield at Hastings; the strong shield.

One day I had seen several massive, dark trees hauled to the Fortescue Estate saw mills, to be sawn into gateposts and lengths for fencing, and I had asked if I might buy them and have them sawn into planks. The forester agreed, and there they were, laid on battens in the corn barn, the playground of rats during the years they stood there. Should we sell them? Would I ever be able to set up my carpenter's bench again, and occupy myself with set-saw and plane, chisel, and dowel-pin?

"Why not?" Loetitia asked. "Yes, let's keep the lovely pink planks!" Her enthusiasm made me keen again, and I said I would not sell them though the auctioneer declared that many would be after them, if he advertised them in his catalogue.

"Besides," said Loetitia, "John and Robert and Richard are growing up, and one of them might turn out to be a farmer, and there are other farms in England. But not just yet!" she laughed. "No farms for the next year or two, at any rate!"

I decided not to attend the auction; it would be too much of an anticlimax. But on the day I went through with it all. I was glad that I did, for many small farmers came to buy, and it was pleasing to find that several came to me to learn what condition this or that implement was in; and I told them the facts, which they accepted. It is good to be trusted by one's fellows; indeed, life without trust is not worth living.

At last all was cleared up, but it took weeks. The last trailer-load drawn behind the old Silver Eagle was unloaded at the new place; the last eight-ton load of matured logs thrown off in the yard by the garage; the stacks of straw, hay and heaps of farmyard dung and the growing crops valued, and the new farmer settled in our farmhouse.

Our furniture, bit by bit, was installed in the roomier house in Suffolk; the logs burning redly in the new, open hearth; beehives set against the wall and hens in the new wire enclosure in the new garden, the old weeds already being trodden down and the earth scratched; the sacks of tail-corn stood in corridor and corner, the cars in the garage and the doors locked. At last we were in the new home.

My intuition on first seeing it, when the Silver Eagle had broken down in an unknown village months before, had not been false. We loved the house, its oak floors, clean walls, its kitchen and scullery, its bathroom and bedrooms, and its space to move about in. And when the children came home for the Christmas holidays, what fun we had, playing hide-and-seek in the evenings!

IX

The kitchen in the new house was panelled in varnished pine and we decided, as it was winter, to have our meals in there. The coal stove looked to be fairly modern, and although the room was dark – with only one window facing north – when the midday sun shone, the light was reflected from the white brick wall opposite.

In the morning we sat down to breakfast under electric light. When building is freed again, we said, we will have a row of glass tiles let into the southern slope of the roof, and so be able to sit in a flood of early sun.

Some kind friends had come over early on the day we arrived to warm the house for us. They had brought over a basket of sticks, and some coal with which to light the kitchen range. When we got there, we found two apologetic ladies wondering what they had done wrong; for smoke poured out of the grate. The chimney had been swept previously, and the flues of the range cleaned.

In the dim, eclipsed light of the electric bulb I saw their distressed faces through the murk of floating smuts, and heard their cries of "Something appears to be wrong!" All their good intentions, of having a warm and bright fire for us, and a kettle singing on the hob, had gone up in smoke!

I tried not to think of the new distemper of the kitchen above the line of panelling, and the clean white ceiling, for sensitive people often "get" our thoughts, however much we dissemble. The point was that I fancied myself as knowledgeable on stoves and fires, and so, taking off my coat, I advanced towards the smoking furnace.

How long had it been like that? Oh, for about an hour, ever since they had lit the fire. I tried not to think, then why didn't you put the beastly fire out, for that would have been rank ingratitude; and after all, they had come several miles to do us this kindness. They thought it must be the chimney. The first thing I saw was the open door of a kind of flue which pivoted just above the level of the stove, probably for an open fire. It was set hard in rust, and when we tried to shut it, it wouldn't budge, so we thought it was designed like that.

"I am afraid you have had a lot of trouble," said Loetitia. "It was so kind of you to come over. Would you like some tea? I've got the electric kettle here."

Our kind helpers had brought milk and cups, in case ours were not unpacked, and while I struggled with the set-fast flue-door, they went into the next room and left me, at my request, to it. The little boys looked on. Orders were shot at them.

"Rikky, fetch the hammer and tinsmith's shears from my mobile box of tools in the Silver Eagle. Robbie, look about in the garden for a largish tin, from which I can cut a strip to fill this gap. Ten inches by three inches."

"Yes, sir."

"Yes, sir."

Rikky, still wearing the coalminer's helmet, departed with Robbie. I called Rikky back.

"Bring pincers first. Quickly!"

"Yes, sir."

Digging his heels imaginatively into an imaginary pony, Rikky cantered off to the old car standing in the adjacent yard. He galloped back with the tools.

Soon the split-pin of the iron rod on which the flue-door was supposed to hinge was drawn, and the door removed. Flames and soot now poured out of an opening ten inches by three inches. Ah, an idea! Outside, by a patch of frost-withered nettles, I had noticed a small rusty iron plate which I recognised as once being the nameplate on a farm-cart. I ran to get it, nearly bumping into Robbie ambling towards the open kitchen door with the remains of a rusty pail, from which the bottom had long since fallen away, in his hand.

"This is all I can find," he announced, when Rikky hurried past him, carrying the rusty plate I had gone to seek.

"Dope!" cried Rikky, regarding the tattered pail fragments. "What's the use of that daft thing?"

"You tell me," suggested Robbie with a toothy grin and merry smile.

"Don't grin, boy!" cried Rikky, his brown eyes smouldering. "Do you want all the new distemper spoiled?"

"I'm afraid the pail's not much good," I said. "Rikky has found the very thing I just thought of."

"Look, Dad," said Rikky, "it's got a Norfolk name on it."

"T. Gotobed, Lynn," spelled Robbie. "Coo, that little old tumbril did some travelling, to come all the way down here to Suffolk."

"Well, Norfolk's only just over the border," said Rikky, adding, "Dope!"

We went into the kitchen. The nameplate fitted exactly over the flaming rectangle. No more smoke came out. I fixed it to the chimney pipe with some old wireless flex, then turned to open the window and fell over the rusty pail which Robbie had left, like an obedient retriever, beside me.

That night Loetlla, after a hot bath, came into the room where I was sitting with the boys before the fire in the open hearth, and said she liked the house. Robbie was making toast over the flammeous embers of thorn and ash logs; and we all had a bacon sandwich and coffee, while listening to Tommy Handley on the radio.

The furniture van was returning with another load on the morrow, and I was also going to the old home to get another load for Silver Eagle and trailer. The thought of it was oppressive; but "littles by littles" as they said in East Anglia. It was to take me six months before I was free of the feelings of self-disgrace at leaving my land.

Meanwhile, Robbie and Rikky were sleeping in the attic room on the second floor. About midnight I peeped in, to find them, as I thought, sleeping. While on my way to my bedroom I heard the snarl of an amorous cat, and glancing through the lattice window, I saw a shadowy shape pursuing another across the road. Soon another skirling snarl arose into the night, and looking out of the window again, I saw three or four shadows moving on the pavement below. Far-away a melancholy crooning came from an old tom who felt out of it.

The singing of country cats at such times is not so violent or prolonged as among town cats who, generally speaking, do no work for their livings, and therefore have an excess of time, energy, or emotion. Country cats spend much of their time hunting rats and waiting for mice, and they are not quite so prone to those thwarted feelings which produce crooning.

I was musing on the fundamental characteristics of all mammals when a strange object swished past my head, followed by what appeared to be a rope or thick piece of string; for the electric lamps over the village street were not yet extinguished. There was a clattering on the cobbled pavement below, and several cat-forms fleeing in all directions away from the base of our new house. A boyish voice whispered in the obscurity above me, "Cor, that's made 'em scram," while a delighted giggling told me that the two comedians, Robbie and Rikky, were at their games. The object was drawn up past my head – the broken pail.

X

The children soon found that the new house was a wonderful place through which to play hide-and-seek. There were so many rooms and passages; two cellars and four sets of stairs, six if the oak-and-brick cellar steps were counted.

You could also climb up through a small trap-door in the ceiling of the garret room; go for a long way under the oaken rafters, and hear the wind moaning and whispering under the slate roof. But that place, most mysterious with its brick chimney-breasts and dark corners which might hide owls, bats, or even ghosts, was out of bounds; for the electric wires stretched in all directions and they might kill you.

Likewise Father had warned the children against trying to touch the electric cables which passed outside their bedroom window with stick or string and especially the thin, steel fly-rod which had come from Canada.

The cellars, too, were not to be used for hide-and-seek, as they were hung with long, black cobwebs. The game was a fast one, being chased up and down the various stairs and through the rooms. Usually Father chased John, Robbie, and Rikky; but sometimes they chased Father. It wasn't fair to split up, for then it would be too easy; they must keep together, and Father promised not to run too fast, for Rikky's legs were short, and if he ran too fast he might fall down the stairs or even go hurtling over the banisters.

Nearly every night for the first week in the new house they played hide-and-seek. There were many places in which to hide, then to slip out and dash away with a ringing "Ha, ha!" to the pursuers. For three nights the boys were puzzled, for Father seemed to be two people at once.

They couldn't make it out. One moment he was locked in the bank room, and John had the key to the only door into the bank. They saw him lying on the floor, behind the high stool, and they guarded the door; and the next moment they heard the sinister "Ha, ha!" behind them, and dashing past Mother, who was quietly knitting by the wood fire, they saw his legs disappearing round the turn of the main stairway. How did that happen? They could hardly sleep at night for trying to puzzle it out among themselves.

Now the bank room led off from the sitting-room by a narrow passage, with a small window looking on to the main street. About a hundred years ago, the owner of the house was also a banker, and to do his business he went through the short passage, opened the door, and was in the bank. There was another door, leading to the street, but that was locked when customers had gone for the day. Then the banker came into the house by the passage, locked the door behind him, entered through another door (which also was locked) into the living or sitting-room with its open fireplace.

About sixty years before we moved into the house the banker had sold his business to another bank, which in turn had merged into a larger bank, and that bank, after some years, had become the great concern which now came out once a week for a few hours from the market town five miles away, and did business with the villagers. The bank rented the room from us, and we had to keep it clean and light a fire every Wednesday, which was its day of business.

Now how did Father get out of the bank room? They knew how he got in, for they saw him running in, past Mother. There was only one door, that into the narrow passage, and John had the key to that. When they ran out into the street, and shone a torch through the glass windows, which would not open, they saw his feet behind the tall old-fashioned desk. They dashed back to the passage again, through the front door and the hall, and so into the sitting-room, and they heard him inside the bank; and the next minute, a bell jangled loudly on its curved spring, and there he was, leaping up the stairs.

"Come on, Dad, tell us how you got out? Oh, come on! No, you didn't get through a secret trap-door in the floor, because you didn't lift up the oilcloth! We know there is a cellar under the bank, but Rikky guarded the cellar door, and it was shut all the time; then the bell jangled just inside the cellar, and you cried 'Ha, ha!' then you were leaping up the stairs behind Rikky's back! Come on, tell us how you did it!"

"It's really very simple, like all mysteries, once you know the answer. You try to do it, when its my turn to chase after you!"

It was quite simple. The boys did not know that Father had the key to the street door of the bank. While they ran back from peering in through the glass windows, Father leapt up, opened the street door, ran round the back through the gates leading to the garage and the great wood-pile, through the garden gate, and into the kitchen; there he reached up, tugged at a half-wheel near the ceiling, whitewashed over and unseen, dashed through the door into the hall, and so up the main stairway.

"Oh, that isn't fair because we didn't know you had the key to the front door of the bank!"

"Right! Now find me this time, and you can have the key of the front door of the bank."

Pulling a chair between himself and the boys, Father dashed away, slamming doors behind him, while Mother looked up and listened to hear if the baby would be awakened by all the noise.

Into the dark kitchen; through the door to the back stairs; bang, bang, bang of hands on bare boards, to sound like feet thudding upwards; then nipping back, opening the cellar door just outside the kitchen door, and pulling it to, just as three boys, torch-lights flashing, thudded up the stairs. Then into a small tunnel above the cellar stairs, behind a small door; and Father was hidden right under the stairs.

A muffled "Ha, ha!" came up to where, on the first landing, the boys stood listening.

"Quick, he's down in the kitchen!"

Thudding down again; standing by the open door listening; again, faintly muffled, "Ha, ha!"

"He's upstairs! No, no, quick, listen, he's in the cellar! Ooh, I dursent go in there!"

"It's okay, Rikky, there's only cobwebs there. Look, you wait here, I'll go down. You watch! Funny, he isn't in the cellar. Then where is he?"

"Ha, ha!"

"Right under our feet! He's just under these boards! Oo-er, a secret tunnel!" cried Rikky.

"No, I know, he's in that cupboard in the cellar!" cried John, and they dashed down, to catch Father, covered with cobwebs, as he was about to run out of the cellar.

"Coo, I like this house, its sporty," said Rikky with glee, eating whole-wheat bread-and-dripping, and drinking cocoa with the others before the fire, a few minutes later.

"The only thing I don't like is those toughs outside," said Robbie. "They are waiting to beat us up, one day."

"Let them try," said John.

"No, reprisals are no good," said Father. "I'll talk to them."

"You see," said Mother, later when the boys were in bed, "it is all right so long as Robbie and John are home; but Rikky by himself is afraid to go out in the street."

"Has he cheeked them?"

"Oh no, Rikky never cheeks anyone! They are just three rough boys, about thirteen, and I fancy they come from difficult homes. But it's not fair that Rikky should be so scared."

Father said he would stop all that; and began to think out a line of action. He switched on the radio, and the wonderful music of Sibelius filled the room. He switched off the light, and they sat in the firelight until the music was over, and it was time for bed.

XI

The lattice windows of my writing-room are frail; the old glass panes are loose in the thin lead ribbons attached to the rusty iron frame. In the summer breeze which wanders across the garden the casements tremble and tinkle faintly. I like to hear the chimmer of the glass loose in the lead casing, to see the clouds passing slowly in the sky, to pause in my writing and see the swallows chasing one another over the tiled roofs of the village.

Down in the garden, Baby Sarah totters after the tortoiseshell cat, crooning to herself, "Oh, burr! burr!"

Burr is anything and everything that the yearling child loves. A covey of partridges in the field of mown hay, a chestnut Suffolk horse coming in to stable after the day's work with the team-man, a dead rabbit lying by the gateway of the farm opposite our house – where Sarah passes every day, strapped kneeling in her pram, and leaning out and over to watch everything with her large grey eyes – a chaffinch on a spray of the hawthorn hedge, a blue butterfly over the barley, even an ant on her shoe, which she scrutinises gravely while exploring on the lawn – all these excite the tender delight of this mite born into the world when phosphorus was burning and choking hundreds of thousands in German cities; and gas and flame were absorbing the ultimate cries of many more in concentration camps.

Each one could be a Jesus mild;
Each one has been a little child;

wrote John Masefield in his startling and beautiful poem, *The Everlasting Mercy*, at the beginning of this twentieth century of alleged progress.

What will the world into which she was born do to the heart and mind of small Sarah?

There is no doubt in my mind that we get the world that we deserve: that the world as we know it is made by ourselves. I am the architect of my own small and personal fortune or disaster.

For many years I was not my own architect. I was, in my early years, an echoing box of what I heard about me, what I read, what I unconsciously absorbed from my early environment.

When I found out, or thought I found out, how wrong and narrow and partisan that world was, I rejected it, and set out alone to make my own world, in the remote country. As a crank and an eccentric – saying and thinking differently from other people – I saw, during the succeeding years, another war being prepared in the mental attitudes of most of those about me; but I could not prove it. I cannot prove it to-day; and even as I write this, I hardly know how to continue.

If I were to write as truly as I feel, would it be acceptable?

On my desk is something I cut out of a newspaper a few weeks ago. I have read it many times since. I saw it first at the end of last April. It is the utterance of a great man:

> Ordinary folk of every country show themselves kindly and brave and serviceable to their fellow-men, but are driven against one another by forces and organisations and doctrines as wantonly and remorselessly as they ever were in the ages of absolute emperors and kings . . . the psychic energies of mankind have been exhausted by the tribulations through which they have passed, and are still passing. It is not only blood-letting which has weakened and whitened us. The vital springs of human inspiration are, for the moment, drained.

It is the utterance of a wise man. Now I do not judge a man great or wise by his politics, but by his courage and integrity, and by his power of mind to embrace much more than a partisan sympathy. I rejoice in

Winston Churchill's words because within myself I know that the only hope of the world of humanity is in men abdicating their own selfishness and thereby in seeing others as they see themselves.

Men to-day all over the world suffer from a sense of injustice. They feel that it is the other man, the other side, which has been unjust to them. But the way to clarity and understanding lies in thinking how one may have been unjust to others; not merely in feeling the injustice done to oneself.

That is the old way, the Old Testament; the alternative is the New Testament. I am not a churchman, and I do not know what religion I "believe in," unless it is in all religions which are true, in that they lead a man out of the old partisan consciousness which eventually drains the "vital springs of human inspiration," to the new pathway where the vital springs of human inspiration are *filled*.

You must forgive me if I write about my own feelings, about myself so much. This is because I only know myself; and by trying truly to know myself, during many hours of meditation, I may thereby be able to know my fellow-man.

Thus, in a small thing – a man bumps into me in the street, and if I did not think before speaking I might say, "Why the hell don't you look where you are going?" Instead, I say, if I think first, "I am so sorry!" Then he may think, and possibly say, as he hurries on, "My fault!"

He may be bumped into later on, by someone whose mind is also filled with an urgent problem, and think to say, in his turn, that he is sorry.

Now why should a man say he is sorry, even if he imagines that the error or fault was not his? Why should he, to use a metaphor to be found in the New Testament, "turn the other cheek?"

Well, it is because he knows that he has bumped into people in the past, when hurrying somewhere and perhaps with an urgent mission – urgent to him, that is. He is sympathetic to those who may be in a jam, or het-up, because he has himself been het-up, and therefore he understands those who are similarly beset. So, using his knowledge, such as it is, he does his best to make the other man feel easier, and therefore he apologises first. This is a trivial example of what all the true seers and poets and artists of the world know to be the only way of living.

There comes to mind a major example of the magnanimous

treatment of others, which was applied to our "enemies" after the Boer War; with the result that Jan Smuts to-day holds the highest military rank in the British Army, a fact that honours both South Africa and our own country.

Is this a long way from Baby Sarah, sitting down there on the lawn, beaming over a cranefly just emerged from its pupal sheath among the rootlets of the grasses?

"Oh, burr!" cries Sarah, seeing not an insect-pest, but a marvellous creature with delicate wings and long slender legs, towards whom she is entirely benevolent, as can be observed in her action of holding out to it the remains of the crust she has just taken out of her mouth.

XII

As we walked round the lanes of Suffolk, myself pushing the pram with Baby Sarah in order to get extra exercise, Loetitia walking beside me, and Rikky riding ahead on his new bicycle – earned by excellent gardening and faithful feeding of hens, without supervision or need to remind the ten-year-old that it was his job and duty – looking for new nests, I had time and mental freedom to observe, with pleasure, the work of other farmers.

Near our new house is a large lake, and beside the lake is a barbed-wire camp for prisoners of war. The Italians were all gone as the first year of the armistice ended, and their place was taken by Germans.

Every morning at 7 a.m. the lorries taking them to work in the fields thundered past our house, and about 5 p.m. they returned, long convoys of them. Walking round the countryside, I saw what they had done.

The sight was, to me, most pleasing. Gone were the choked ditches and field-drains of peace-time, the overgrown hedges, the rush-clumps in the sodden fields of grass choked by moss. Now the hedges had been cut to the stub, and the new ruddy shoots of thorn, green sprays of the ash and wild plum, were growing up again. The ditches were deep, the sides slanting and smoothed and water reflected the sky five feet lower than it had in the bad old days before the war – when it had lain in the unploughed fields.

Now the arable tradition of Suffolk was restored; the fields of heavy dark-brown clay were rich with wheat, barley, oats, and parallel lines of sugar-beet plants. And when the May blossom was turning rusty, the beans came into flower, and the warm air was filled with the soft honey-scent of their fragrance. And such good crops, too!

It was a pleasing sight, and it seemed to me that we had come to a district which was one of the best-farmed in the whole of England.

The hedges which had looked somewhat naked after the cutting-back were springing up again with new shoots, as I have said; and in the nettles and umbelliferous plants many small birds were singing and perching.

Rikky told me that he had already found forty-three nests; he spent all his leisure time looking for new ones, and visiting those already found. He went alone, for the native boys did not appear to share his passion for watching birds; and too often we saw nests that had been pulled out, and thrown on the ground, after the eggs had been taken. One made me angry, for we had watched it being built in a blackthorn thicket: a long-tailed tit's nest, moulded of spiders' webs and lichen into the shape of a coconut, and lined with over a thousand feathers, each borne by one or other of the birds, from a distant farmyard where hens lived. In the winds of early April, the bearing of a feather in the tiny beaks of these minute birds had been a problem, for sometimes the wind-resistance against the feather was greater than the wing-power of the little grey bird.

Rikky had watched the birds building their home, and seen them, at sunset, creeping into their domed nest, folding their long tails over their backs, and squatting side by side. Such fidelity, such rapture, as the white fragile eggs were laid – each scarcely bigger than a pea – and every visitation by a human being, or footsteps passing in the lane, causing their hearts to beat rapidly; for birds are very nervous, always alert for danger.

Rikky knew all this; and when one morning he found the nest lying broken on the ground, its feathers scattered, and no sweet small *chee-chee, chee-chee* being whispered in the oak over the thorn-thicket, he went pale, and walked away, muttering he would not go there again.

I have often noticed that in villages where there is an old-fashioned (or it may be stupid) schoolmaster, who relies on fear and the cane to keep order, to eke out his sparse knowledge and confidence, the boys are usually rough and "tough." I know nothing about the local schools; but I do know that in one village wherein I lived, the children swore a lot, bullied one another, jeered, and generally were not as they might have been.

The school was in charge of an old spinster; and when a new mistress came, a friendly and able young woman, within a month the entire mental outlook of the children was altered. They entered the school in the mornings to the playing of a gramophone; they were eager to hear what teacher wanted to tell them, in her own simple and keen way; they learned to act and sing together; they were encouraged to be unafraid; and soon it was apparent that a miracle had been wrought in their outlook.

If they passed you in the street, and you said, "Good-morning," they did not giggle, or look astonished; they were your friends, and you felt you were theirs. And soon no more picked and cast-away flowers were to be seen lying in the village street; clothes looked tidier, and shoes were clean on going to school; and the grown-ups went about their work feeling that life was going to be better.

Twice a year parents were invited to the school to see the little plays and to hear the singing and the recitation of poems by Thomas Hardy, Walter de la Mare, Shelley, and other poets, who in simple words had crystallized the beauty and the truth of life, which these people were now beginning to realise.

For it had been a difficult village, before the war, so many had been out of work, and the fields were neglected and overgrown with weeds. There was no squire and the church was empty on Sundays; people did not go, for there was nothing there to hear that moved their imaginations. Jesus of Nazareth drew the multitudes because He both knew and could express the Truth which is so often locked away in a lonely, or frustrated, heart.

Our walks down the lanes of Suffolk every afternoon brought back to me those days when, in another village, I knew every tree, nest, grass, field, bird and animal. Now Rikky was doing and feeling what I used to feel, and I was content. And what nests did he find! There was a great crested grebe by the mere; a blackcap warbler in some brambles; a lesser spotted woodpecker in an old decayed tree, and many tomtits, robins, hedge-sparrows, thrushes and blackbirds.

Sometimes I went with him farther afield, and we saw the two boys who "pulled" nests. I showed Rikky how to cover his tracks, to lift brambles pressed down by his feet, to lift green nettles and grasses bent over by his passing. We found where the long-tailed titmice were building a second nest, and agreed not to go near it, in case he was watched.

It was sweet to linger by a gatepost, on which the remnants of an old hand-made oaken gate hung – relic of the glory of farming in an age before the machine had dominated mankind – and listen to the birds singing, and to look up into the blue sky which no longer echoed with the thunder of the bombers by day and by night; and to think of a new age, perhaps when one has passed on, when no wild birds' nests will be torn out of English hedgerows, because all boys will have a fair beginning at home, at school, and in a working life.

XIII

My small boy, Richard, does not read these meditations, or confessions, that I write every fortnight in my quest for harmony or truth, so I can write about him without embarrassing him. Anyway, the truth should not be embarrassing to anyone who is "clear." By "clear" I mean one without mental fear. A child with mental fear is a haunted child. He or she has been tried beyond his present capacity.

For example, a child may be frightened of the water because he has been introduced to water in the wrong manner. Water is one of the elements which again are the makers of all life. Take a wee bairn to a puddle and see how he delights in it, how he plays and splashes without mental fear. But take a small boy for the first time to a long, blue shimmering swimming bath, and throw him in, and he may be frightened of water all his life, unless he grows out of the fear by a later familiarity with water. Idiots used to do such things with small boys; hence brutality, which springs from mental fear.

Rikky, from his earliest years, has had affection and stability in his life. He was the youngest of five; he had at least five friends in the world the moment he was born. They encouraged his earliest impressions of life with smiles and tender attentions. Five pairs of hands were ready to save him if he tottered; to pick him up and soothe him were he to fall and hurt himself.

Then there was, of course, Mum-mum, who later became Mummie, then Mother. There was also Dad-dad. The first coherent cry of a baby is Dad-dad – possibly arising from teeth coming from soft gums and the instinct to bite on them – which all mothers encourage the baby to identify with his male parent, especially when the mother is in love with the one who has given her her child. Dad-

dad became Dad, then Father, occasionally Henry, and then a steady Dad.

Dad might at times be a bit "tisky" with the elder boys, but always with Rikky he was amenable and ready to sympathise.

Father, from his point of view – and his view-point was as true to him as was Rikky's to Rikky – liked Rikky because he found in the small, dark-eyed child a beautiful sense of clarity, or truth. When Rikky declared that a thing was so, it was so. To Rikky a spade was a spade, for digging soil over; a shovel was a shovel, for removing soil or gravel already dug by pick or spade.

There were on the farm several kinds of spade: the long-handled, narrow, sharp spade for cutting the clayed sides of ditches nice and even; the heart-shaped spade with a curved swan-neck for lifting up turf; the very narrow ferreting spade, for digging out a "fitchey" which had lain up after feasting on a rabbit.

Then the shovels were various; the wooden shovel for heaping up loose and light chaffed hay in the hay barn; the thicker wooden shovel for turning over barley in the corn barn, lest it "heat" and grow mouldy before it was sacked up and sent away to the maltster, who had bought it by sample shown by father in the Corn Hall of Norwich; the sand shovel for chucking up fine building sand in the lorries; and others for various purposes. Richard knew each one after he had watched it being worked.

He called a spade a spade, and not a shovel; certainly he had not the kind of education which would call it an implemental stratum disturber, or a ruddy backbreaker.

For at an early age Rikky learnt to use his muscles in digging; and he liked digging. See his garden to-day, about thirty square yards of soil set with peas and beans, rows of cabbages and onions and lettuces, with its little compost heap and its few flowers on the border. Digging at the right time; hoeing when the weeds were tiny, and no trouble; proper seed-beds made before the seed was carefully sown home. Why not?

Why, indeed, should any child grow up to hate work, if that work be seen by him in his early years as something interesting, vital and proper? No compulsion, no "come on now, get on with it."

Rikky is his own master; he is almost master of himself. I say almost, because he is still liable, but on rare occasions, to feel affronted and hurt, due to an excessive sensibility, and then his life can coil back upon him with a terrifying frustration which diminishes his eyes and makes them dark and burning, where before they were large and luminous, filled with warm interest for all living things. What is the cause of that? Just a slight trace of the "mother" complex which he is outgrowing.

His mother gives all her consideration and thought to the children; for the marriage of "true minds," in Shakespeare's phrase, is rare on this earth. But the balance of father's rough, male friendliness is enough to give Rikky balance, so that when he goes to boarding-school after the summer, he will go, not a boy with strangulated feelings because he is leaving his mother, but as a young man keen to enjoy the new life, which he hopes will be fun, as it will be if in the Marches of the West he finds birds which are not common in the East, such as raven and kite, buzzard and peregrine falcon.

Such a boy, brought up in balance between his father and his mother – learning to trust his sensitive feelings from his mother and his fleetness of body and his own calm thoughts from his father – will have a proper chance in life.

He will not "flap" in a difficult situation; he will, one hopes, find a balance between what Walpole expressed in the famous phrase, "Life is a tragedy to those who feel, and a comedy to those who think." Why should he be bored, with his interest in racing motorcars, tractors, birds, animals, fish, postage stamps, pictures, drawing, music, plays, and comics like Mr. Thomas Handley?

And won't a child, brought up in balance between parents – whether a girl, giving to each a corresponding development of affection of herself, or a boy, likewise poised in emotion between mother and father – have the best chance of a happy marriage, and a following happy parenthood?

Such a plain or simple outlook on life is not likely to lead an adolescent or youth into a camouflaged erotic or false sentimentality about the one he or she suddenly, after that little piercing pain between the ribs, finds very important in life, terribly real and disturbing – oh, so deliciously and poignantly – to a life hitherto carefree and independent.

Clarity is truth; to see plain is to see the truth; to learn to use words plainly is to tell the truth. And was is not said by one of the greatest of all poets – and the most homeless – that only the truth can make one whole?

No, young Rikky, of whom I am privileged to be part of his physical creation, will not be embarrassed by this article, should his quiet eye fall on it.

XIV

I read in the newspaper the other day about a boy of nine being caned because, at school, he could not repeat the letters of the alphabet. About that time I was staying with a friend who has a boy of fifteen at a public school who has caused some consternation in his family by stealing. Two days later I was visiting another friend, who has a remarkably robust little girl of three. She spent some part of the afternoon in pushing a handful of straw at my eyes as I lay on the lawn; and when I moved away she pursued me, with a sort of gleeful laugh, to where I had gone behind an apple tree, and threw hard pieces of sun-baked clay at me.

Her mother was firm with her – "Mustn't give way to a child" – and there ensued a sort of struggle of wills between the adult woman and the small female child. The mother, whose spirit is as strong as her daughter's, won; the child was sent indoors howling. She came back later on, smiling a peculiar smile, and once again I moved away.

Grandfather, working hard in the garden, after a week in a London office, looked up and said to me grimly, "You sentimentalists would let her get on with it, wouldn't you? Do you know why her mother is such a fine woman? Because I brought her up the way she should go. When I took my boy to his public school, I watched the games-master at the nets, coaching the boys. He didn't know I was looking on. I heard him lamming into them. When he passed me later, he said, 'May I help you, sir, in anything?' I replied that I was a prospective parent getting the feel of the place, before deciding to send my boy there. He looked a bit startled. 'I was listening to you just now,' I went on. 'I heard what you were saying.' 'Oh, really, sir, at times one lets fly, I admit –' he began apologetically, when I broke in with, 'Don't worry, son. I heard enough to decide to send my boy here! You win!' He grinned, and I went back and told the Headmaster I hoped my boy would pass the entrance examination. He was down for two other schools, in case he failed at any one, you know."

His daughter, the mother of the small girl, had breakfast with me the next morning, before the grandfather appeared. The small girl sat at the table. The mother is soft-voiced, cool, and one of the ablest of women under thirty at her particular work. I cannot tell you what the job is, for it would be tantamount to telling her name, which is fairly well known. The point is that she possesses cool courage, and a poise of mind and body which is rare, in either man or woman; she has a gentle touch, a factual mind, and a sensitivity which shows in her work and in her appreciation of all true art; but, in my opinion, she has wrong ideas – derived from her father – of how to treat children.

While we ate wheatmeal bread and butter with honey for breakfast, we spoke in quiet voices, in tune with each other, and the small girl sat there akin to our mood. She was quiet and composed; she was herself; entirely different from the distraught wildling of the aggressive ego of the day before. But when her grandfather appeared, and rated her for beginning to get jittery and discomposed, she stuck out her underlip, her eyes hardened, and . . . but you will know the rest. It became a conflict of wills again, the small plastic brat *versus* the matured human being.

Curiously, man, woman and child all had the same quality of forthright, as they had the same wide-spaced blue eyes. What was wrong? Something was wrong; for when a small child becomes a nuisance, it is because something is wrong. A motor engine, boiling and spluttering, is out of adjustment; it was not designed or made to boil, to fail to pull its load, to give trouble, to be cursed, to be the cause of disharmony.

Now for a moment let us return to the boy at his public school who stole something belonging to his best friend, and who almost flaunted it when he went home at half-term. His father, a kindly man, but one whose mind was formed in the old school – he was a subaltern in the South African war – disliked his elder son, as he adored his younger son. The elder boy could do little right; the younger boy, little wrong. There was love and affection between Father and his younger boy; there was lack of love between Father and the elder boy. It had been so, growing worse, ever since the younger boy appeared.

The father was twenty years older than his wife; and I knew there had never been a true flow of love between them. Desire, yes; affection, yes; frustration, certainly. It was a common situation; for many men grow to maturity without ever experiencing that rare thing, the harmony and benison of true love. There is no substitute for true love. I write true love, because "love" has many forms; but true love is one and indivisible with liking; wishing to be with the beloved, feeling life is incomplete without his or her company; and true love is stronger than death, and the only source of harmony.

Father and mother were not in balance; they remained together because they were the decent sort of people who try to make the best of life, and who have a reticence about the things of the interior heart. The elder boy was the product of that disharmony. Ignorant of his lonely feelings, fearful of his father who could not help resenting the love of his young wife for her child – the father feeling the baby had come between them – the boy grew up in an atmosphere of constraint. He was afraid of the big fellow who was his father.

So, lonely and disprized, the boy becomes an exhibitionist, in his own way. With a fearful, interior fascination, due to his being at odds with life, he finds some sort of false justification in doing what he knows is wrong, what he knows he will be punished for, with a hopeless dullness of inevitable disaster, he steals; and he does not trouble to conceal the fact. Indeed, he lays himself open to being detected by his father.

What is the cure of the cause of "stealing?" Is it in driving the iron of misprision deeper into his soul, by punishment, by thrashing him, by making him feel he is done for, before he starts life? Such a boy, a year or two ago, were he old enough, might run away and try to join the army, driven by a hidden death-wish; instinctively to find, in oblivion, the tenderness and understanding which he, in mournful aloneness, did not find in life. All the mother's love in the world does not compensate for the frowns and voided affection of a father. Love, security, and understanding, that is what all children, who are helpless to plead for themselves, need if they are to grow into the kind of people whose moral integrity is above the mass-maladjustment which prepares the psychosis of modern wars.

Now for the small boy of nine whose body bore the brown scores of the cane, because he could not remember, or repeat the alphabet: what can be said for him? Indeed, we are back in the dark ages; indeed, for the moment the world has lost the true values of life. I have been that small boy; I have been caned because I could not learn. No, I would not cane the schoolmaster, or its equivalent, for caning a small boy.

You cannot cure the world's maladjustment by bombing those who drop bombs; by burning those who burn others. That is merely an eye for an eye; that is revenge masking itself as moral indignation. We have all got to learn the truth from those whose gifts and experiences fit them to tell the truth; and the core of all truth, in its many variations, is to be found in the New Testament.

XV

It is early morning as I write. The sun shines through the lattice window of my bedroom. Over the road an acacia tree waves its feathery green leaves in a gentle wind that scarcely shakes the web which a spider is spinning across the space of my open casement window. The day will be fine and hot – a wonderful day for my journey down into Devon.

The car stands below in the garage, ready packed. Now this time is the climax of a week's anxieties; would the car be ready in time for the journey?

For we are all going to have a holiday together, in a field on a hilltop in Devon overlooking the sea, in tents, huts and bivouacs. The first real holiday since before the war, for while we were farming there were no holidays in the summer. It was all hard work in hayfield and harvest field.

For weeks we have been working on the small, low, speedy car, with its twin silver exhaust pipes coming through the side of the bonnet. Now all is in order; resleeved engine run in, new gear-box fitted, new springs, shackles for springs, new silencer, and body-work repaired and the whole resprayed.

Rikky has been helping, and wondering if it will ever be ready, and will we really start on the day we said we would? His flying helmet and goggles have been cleaned several times each day for the past week and put down on the bench ready to be taken up at *the* moment, in the very early morning.

Rikky is the more excited because in our village lives a farmer's son who had a car like ours; and all during the early spring Rikky and other boys used to watch that car being stripped, its parts examined with great care, and the whole being built up again to perfection. The mysterious car lived in a shed up a steep gravelly, narrow lane, beside a small bungalow.

One day the gleaming car, so low on the road, was ready, and the village boys saw it moving away up the village street. A week or two later they heard that that car and driver who had tuned it with such care and precision, had won the Belgian Grand Prix, and that Mr. St. John Horsfall was back again with two silver cups and a thousand pounds! Some of the reflected glory fell on me, when Rikky saw the magic words Aston Martin on the radiator of his father's new car.

The swifts are whistling shrilly down the otherwise silent village street. Far off a cock crows. Some of the leaves of the acacia in the garden opposite now are splashed with light, as the sun rises over the levels of the hedges and flattened corn of the fields up the lane. Dare I write that I am so glad I am not a farmer this year?

It is not really self-congratulation; for having been a farmer I know full well what my neighbours are feeling, after one of the worst summer storms of the century.

Two days ago it happened. We were working on the 2-litre Aston Martin when a pallor spread over the sky out of the south-west, so that for a moment I thought it was autumn, or even winter, and the day was closing in. In the sky great slate quarries were mounting in a livid silence. From the garden I heard the voice of baby Sarah, a little fretful in the oppressing heat. Her mother was away in the town for the day, and I was looking after her. If she were wakeful it would take me from my work, and so much had to be done.

But it wasn't Sarah who disturbed my friend and me, for soon it was too dark to see the nuts under the chassis. The sky was now nearly as dark as a grape; but a petrified grape. It was hard and staring, as though the spirit of life were turning into another dimension. Of course I thought of that damned atom bomb; not that I connected the plumbean hues of the sky directly with it, but it was like the photographs. I asked my friend if he, too, felt "headachey" and tired.

"Yes," he said, "it's the weather. My hat! There's a storm coming."

We decided to push the car into its shed. A kind of silent wind or cold liquid air was now moving sullenly about the garden, shaking leaves, which seemed to whisper anxiously. In the darkling light an owl flew across the garden, and no small birds cried out.

"We ought to shut and bolt the doors," I cried over my shoulder, as I ran into the garden to take the pram with Sarah into the kitchen.

"Come and help me shut the windows," I shouted a minute later from the kitchen, where it had been necessary to switch on the electric light.

The house was dark, as when we used to play hide-and-seek up and down the stairs and through the rooms on winter nights, with only hand torches. As I fastened the flimsy lead-and-glass casement of my upper writing room, with its views over fields and distant woods, I saw the dark slate-quarries of the sky veined with jagged light. Sarah, in my left arm, stared with me. But we could not stand there, with other windows to shut. We went from room to room, while thunder reverberated down the corridors and the stairways.

When we were free to go upstairs again and watch from the window the distant woods were blurred out. The sky quarries were falling as thick grey dust. Before I could light a cigarette I saw the tiled sloping roofs of the lower village smoking white as the wind and rain struck them, the steam arose, only to be swept away. Running to the eastern window I saw the acacia tree over the way being bent to the north, its foliage seething and sweeping in the hurricane which was now pouring past us.

Strangely, there was no noise. The macadamised surface of the broad village street was swept by great sheets of water. Livid light leapt in the room, thunder broke violently, and I thought of the house, which stood on the crest of the hill and had no lightning conductor. And would the tall chimney stack standing out of the kitchen roof seen from the western window fall and smash the kitchen? Those red bricks were old and needed repointing; we could get no one to do the work. Well, if it fell, it fell!

Meanwhile the street, seen from the other window, was rushing in broad wrinkled sheets of water, stained with chalk and gravel.

Hisssh! Crack! That was a near one! The whole house seemed to clap together. Was it a thunderbolt? The roofs were now smoking violently, with rain smashed into mist and flung northwards. I saw the pergola of rambler roses below in the garden simply lean in the same direction, then it was flat. A slate spun through the air and fell on the roadway, to be turned over and over in the sheets of running water, which seemed to be fighting the wind for its possession. It was time to go downstairs, in case the rest of the roof decided to follow the slate.

An hour later the sun shone again. The garage was eight inches deep in water. We took out the car and went on with our work.

And now it is time, to go downstairs and get ready for our journey to the West.

February–October, 1946